*MURDERO

THE PERFECT SAUSAGE

PERFECT

Illustrated by
Philip Reeve

Hippo

To Philip Reeve, without whom most of these books
would have been quite impossible.

Scholastic Children's Books,
Commonwealth House, 1–19 New Oxford Street,
London WC1A 1NU, UK

A division of Scholastic Ltd
London ~ New York ~ Toronto ~ Sydney ~ Auckland
Mexico City ~ New Delhi ~ Hong Kong

Published in the UK by Scholastic Ltd, 2005

Text copyright © Kjartan Poskitt 2005
Illustrations copyright © Philip Reeve 2005

All rights reserved

ISBN 0 439 95901 2

Typeset by MRules
Printed and bound by Nørhaven Paperback A/S, Denmark

2 4 6 8 10 9 7 5 3 1

CONTENTS

*Note: all angles in this book are measured in degrees
and all key formulas are marked with a ★.*

·MURDEROUS **MATHS**.

Join the Murderous Maths gang for more fun, games
and tips at **www.murderousmaths.co.uk**

HOW THIS BOOK CAME TO BE WRITTEN

Once upon a time there was a lazy author who decided to write a book about sausage formulas. He sat down at his desk and typed out all the sausage formulas he could think of (i.e. two of them) and then after three minutes he decided he had done quite enough and went for a lie down feeling very pleased with himself. Before long he had drifted off to sleep and then a dreadful nightmare came to him.

The author woke in a cold sweat. What could he do? How could he ensure that he included all the fundamental formulas that were worth including? It was then that he had a great idea.

So that is what happened. As this book was being written loads of Murderous Maths fans sent in their messages and suggestions for formulas. Some people sent us formulas that were so complicated that we couldn't even understand what they were for, and we certainly couldn't work them out! There were also one or two absolute beauties, just the sort of daft thing that we love, and we got one unprintable formula from two brothers who'd just got a new baby sister which involved bottles of milk consumed, numbers of pats on the back, loudness of burps and the range of her projectile vomit.

So before you dive into this book, we'd like to thank all the people who made suggestions including:

Matt Kimpton and Tom Winch, Steven Charlton, Ana "Sunny" Marin, Michael Jones, Jez McCullough, Steven Watts, David Smith, Alex Jeffreys, Thomas Gooderidge, Hu Yi Jie, Paul Vaartjes, Adam Lane, Stephen Hartwell, Joachim Worthington, Gail Weiss, Tom Wilkinson, Daniel Branch, Ben Sheldon, Tom

Sedgwick, Jordan Watts, N!ck Dec, David Fox, Alasdair Chi, Sanchit Kumar, Ugrid, Sarah Higginson, Monika Dembinska, Jonathan Harris, Georgia Gillard, David Ross Smith, Ian Howard, Kweku Abraham, Daniel Fretwell, Lottie Greenwood, Ian Howard, Jessie BC, Andrew Windsor, Don Berry, Sam Derbyshire, Shanthan Golden, Matthew Sheeran, Benjo Bong, Jeffrey Mei, Jenny Wood, Samuel Walker, Carl Turner, Harry and Charlie Kind (and baby Grace).

** Warning! This list contains at least one teacher and two REAL Pure Mathematicians. **

At least 10 of these people appear in the book. If all else fails – can you find them?

What is a Perfect Sausage?

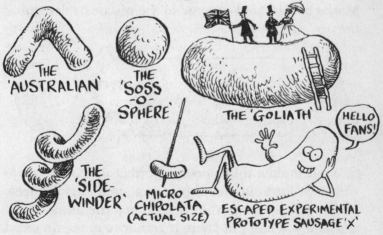

THE 'AUSTRALIAN'

THE 'SOSS -O- SPHERE'

THE 'GOLIATH'

HELLO FANS!

THE 'SIDE-WINDER'

MICRO CHIPOLATA (ACTUAL SIZE)

ESCAPED EXPERIMENTAL PROTOTYPE SAUSAGE 'X'

Over the last 3,000 years, the humble sausage has been adapted by many different civilizations to suit their various cultures. A butcher in Transylvania was famous for his black fang-shaped sausage, while a cook in Yarrowkey, USA, produced the amazing supa-long six-roll frankfurter. There was also the Swiss springing gristle sausage which was used in jack-in-the-boxes, and in Asia archaeologists are still hoping to discover fragments of the mythical Great Seven-Ended sausage that used to stand high across the harbour mouth at Upper Ketchupia.

Everybody agrees that the sausage has made a vital contribution to art, science and culture over the centuries, but there was always one problem. When making these sausages, nobody was ever sure exactly how much sausage skin or filling would be needed because they couldn't work out the volume or the surface area. The measurements of these sausages were always too difficult to take and the sums were too complicated to work out. That's why Murderous Maths has decided to come to the rescue by designing *the perfect sausage*!

What makes this sausage perfect is that it comes with two formulas for the volume and surface area. The way it works is that if you chop the ends off the sausage you can put them together to make an exact ball, and the bit left in the middle is an exact cylinder shape. Thanks to this cunning design, you just need to measure the length and the width of the sausage then put the results into the perfect sausage formulas

8

and get the answers. It's the breakthrough the whole world has been waiting for.

But the world will just have to wait a teeny bit longer because we don't get to the perfect sausage formulas until page 175. Before that we're going to find out exactly what formulas are and how they can sort out money, car chases, tearing up sheets of stamps and how much sugar you need on a doughnut. Remember this:

Formulas don't just sort out sausages, they can sort out your life.

> ### Dear Murderous Maths,
>
> I have only read the first page of your book and already I find myself boiling in fury. Formula is a Latin word and the plural is "formulae" not "formulas". It's thanks to the careless attitude of people like you that the world is in such a mess. You should be ashamed of yourselves. Tut-tut.
>
> Yours snobbishly,
>
> Humphrey Stuckup, Professor of Literature.

Some people should check a dictionary before writing snotty letters. Both *formulae* and *formulas* are in there, and we felt our young and groovy readers would prefer the modern word to the old Latin one. So there.

ALL THE SHAPE AND LUMP FORMULAS YOU'LL PROBABLY EVER NEED

Here are the all-time Top Twelve smash-hit most loved and popular shape and lump formulas that will deal with just about everything you'll ever want…

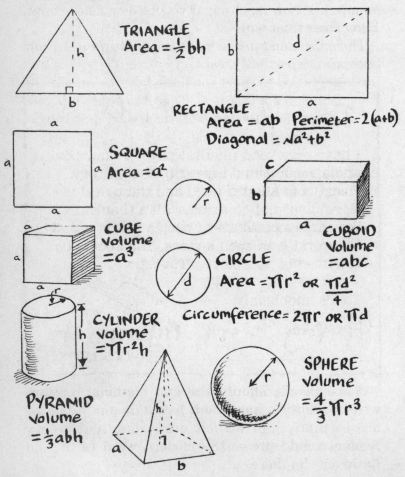

TRIANGLE
Area = $\frac{1}{2}$bh

RECTANGLE
Area = ab   Perimeter = 2(a+b)
Diagonal = $\sqrt{a^2+b^2}$

SQUARE
Area = a^2

CUBE
Volume = a^3

CUBOID
Volume = abc

CIRCLE
Area = πr^2 OR $\frac{\pi d^2}{4}$
Circumference = $2\pi r$ OR πd

CYLINDER
Volume = $\pi r^2 h$

SPHERE
Volume = $\frac{4}{3}\pi r^3$

PYRAMID
Volume = $\frac{1}{3}$abh

If you don't know what to do with these formulas, the rest of this chapter explains what's going on. If you can't see the formula you need here, don't worry. When you've got further into the book and you're a bit older and braver you'll come across another chapter with *all the shape and lump formulas you'll probably NEVER need*.

How formulas work

All a formula does is tell you a list of little sums to do, and most importantly *what order to do them in*. Once you've got used to them you'll see how they make life much simpler. For instance, if you wanted to tell your Auntie Alice how to work out the area of a rectangle, you could put:

Area of a rectangle = the length of a long side × by the length of a short side.

But that's a bit tedious, so what people usually do is draw a little picture like this:

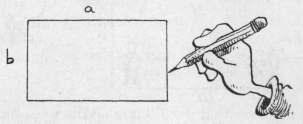

You'll see the different sides are cunningly marked a and b. Now all you need to put is this:

Area of a rectangle = $a \times b$

This is a lot neater, but we're not finished yet. As multiplying is used such a lot in formulas, people quite often miss out the × sign, and just put the two letters together. We end up with:

★ Area of rectangle = *ab*

So if Auntie Alice has a rectangular cow field measuring 30 metres long and 15 metres wide, all she needs to do is swap *a* and *b* for 30 and 15. She will find that the area of her field = 30 × 15 = 450 square metres.

(Areas are always measured in *square* somethings. If you like you can write m^2 for square metres, so this answer would be 450 m^2.)

Now suppose Auntie Alice wants to put a fence all the way around her cow field, how long will it need to be? The distance all the way round a shape is called the **perimeter** and you get it by adding the sides up. Let's draw the field…

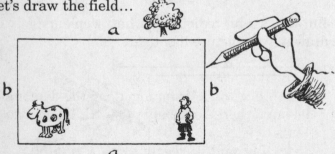

You can see that the distance all the way round is two lots of *a* plus two lots of *b*. We could say the perimeter = 2*a* + 2*b*, but as both bits are multiplied by 2, you can use brackets to write it like this:

★ Perimeter of rectangle = 2(*a* + *b*)

When you have a number outside brackets, it means you have to multiply it by everything inside the brackets. If we put in $a = 30$ and $b = 15$, we get the perimeter = 2(30 + 15).

Here's the most important thing to remember about formulas: when you have brackets *always work out the bit inside the brackets first!* Here the perimeter = 2(45) so then you multiply $2 \times 45 = 90$ metres. That's how long the fence needs to be.

Now let's suppose Auntie Alice suddenly wants to find the shortest path from one corner of the field to the other.

Auntie Alice will be running along the diagonal of the field and there's a formula to work this out too:

$$\star \textbf{ Diagonal of rectangle} = \sqrt{a^2 + b^2}$$

(If you've heard of the ancient Greek mathematician Pythagoras, this formula comes from his famous theorem. And even if you haven't heard of Pythagoras, this formula *still* comes from his theorem and there's nothing you can do about it.)

13

When you see the square root sign $\sqrt{}$ going over a few bits, you treat it like a bracket – so work out everything under the sign before you worry about square rooting anything. We plonk in $a = 30$ and $b = 15$ to get $\sqrt{30^2 + 15^2}$. You always work out powers such as the "squared" things first, which gives us $\sqrt{900 + 225}$. The powers have gone so we can finish inside the bracket to get: $\sqrt{1125}$. Finally there's just the square root to do, and unless you're a genius you reach for your calculator, put in $\sqrt{1125}$ and then tell Auntie Alice the answer:

Of course, it also helps to use a bit of common sense. When somebody is running in a blind panic across a cow field from a giant hand holding a sharp pencil, an answer of 33·5 metres is close enough.

The order of play

By now you'll have realized that it's important to work out the bits of formulas in the right order. If you're in doubt, check this list:

(One thing missing from this list are *trigonometry* bits such as SIN, COS and TAN, but luckily they hardly ever come up. However, when they do, they come in at position $2\frac{1}{2}$ after powers and before × ÷.)

π and circles

Any formula that involves circles will include π. Regular Murderous Maths readers will know all about this cute little sign called "pi" which is equal to 3·1416... but if your calculator has a π button then you don't have to remember this number. Suppose you're wearing your best white trousers and sit on a pickled beetroot, you'll get a nice round purple stain. To work out the area you get a friend to measure the diameter of the stain...

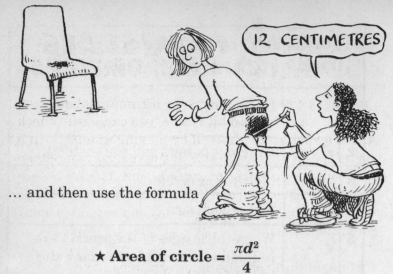

... and then use the formula

$$\star \text{ Area of circle} = \frac{\pi d^2}{4}$$

As $d = 12$ you do the squared bit first, so work out $12^2 = 144$. Next put $144 \times \pi \div 4$ into your calculator and then you can tell the beetroot...

THE AREA OF THAT STAIN IS 113.0973355 cm²

WOW! THAT'S MY PERSONAL BEST!

SELF-SATISFIED GLOW

π is such a groovy thing that it gets a chapter to itself later on, which includes a list of really nasty formulas for working it out. Sadly we have no formulas for working beetroot stains out of white trousers.

NUMBERS, PIZZA SLICES AND ALIEN INTERPRETERS

Maths produces all sorts of strange patterns of numbers and the fun bit is that you can easily check these formulas for yourself by playing around with a set of spheres the same size. If you're a normal person you could use oranges or marbles, but if you're an all-powerful universal deity you could use planets as long as you blow any loose moons and satellites away from them first.

Triangle and tetrahedral numbers

First of all arrange some of your spheres into neat triangle shapes like this:

TRIANGLE: T1   T2   T3   T4

ARRANGEMENT:

NUMBER OF SPHERES   1   3   6   10

Admittedly the first one isn't much of a triangle, but it still counts. The number of spheres in each triangle is the *triangle number*. You'll see the first triangle number (which is normally called T_1 for short) is 1, the second (or T_2) is 3, $T_3 = 6$, $T_4 = 10$ and so on. If you play snooker or pool, you'll have come across the fifth triangle number because both games start with 15 balls in a triangle pattern and $T_5 = 15$.

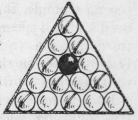

You can go on making your triangles as big as you like and here's how to find out how many spheres you need to make any size of triangle:

★ **The nth triangle number** $T_n = \dfrac{n(n + 1)}{2}$

If you want to know where this formula comes from it's explained in *More Murderous Maths*.

Now we start taking the triangles we've made and pile them up in layers to form a three-sided pyramid.

We start with the first triangle by itself so we just need one sphere. However if we put it on top of the second triangle, the little pyramid we make would need $1 + 3 = 4$ spheres. If we put this pile on top of the third triangle we'd need $1 + 3 + 6 = 10$ spheres. Finally if we put these on top of the fourth triangle we'd need $1 + 3 + 6 + 10 = 20$ spheres.

Each time we're making a bigger and bigger triangular pyramid called a tetrahedron. That's why the series of numbers 1, 4, 10, 20 ... are called tetrahedral numbers.

★ **The nth tetrahedral number** $= \dfrac{n^3 + 3n^2 + 2n}{6}$

(In case you think this formula is a bit useless, you'll find how it can make you £56.20 richer in the "Money!" chapter.)

Centred hexagonal, pentagonal and pyramid numbers

Another series of numbers that comes up in patterns is *centred hexagonal numbers*. The picture says it all...

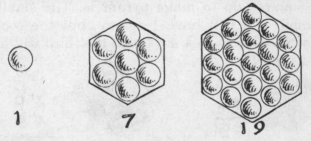

★ **The nth centred hexagonal number** $= 3n^2 - 3n + 1$

You can also have *pentagonal numbers*...

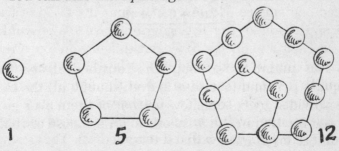

19

★ **The nth pentagonal number** $= \dfrac{n(3n-1)}{2}$

The square numbers are fairly obvious:

★ **The nth square number** $= n^2$

Just as with the triangle numbers, you can stack the squares up to make pyramids. The smallest pyramid will just have 1 sphere, but the second pyramid will have 1 + 4 = 5 and the third will have 1 + 4 + 9 = 14.

★ **The nth square pyramid number**
$$= \frac{2n^3 + 3n^2 + n}{6}$$

The quaint thing about the tetrahedral and the square pyramid formulas is even though all the bits get divided by 6, somehow neither of them ever give you a fraction in the answer. Go on – choose a whole number for n and try it!

These strange sets of numbers link up in all sorts of odd ways. For example, you can always split up any square into two consecutive triangle numbers:

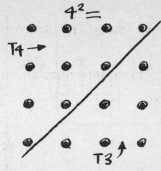

Here you can see that 4^2 = $T_4 + T_3$ and when you convert this to numbers you get 16 = 10 + 6. Here's a little formula to describe what's happening:

$$\star \; n^2 = T_n + T_{(n-1)}$$

These special groups of numbers also have a strange habit of turning up in the most unexpected ways, as you're about to see...

Sheets of stamps

Suppose you have a square sheet of stamps. How many different ways can you make a square shape from it?

If your square sheet of stamps only has 1 stamp, then there's only one way you can make a square. If your square sheet has 2×2 stamps then you can either just leave the big square, or tear out any one of the four little squares: 1 + 4 = 5 ways.

21

③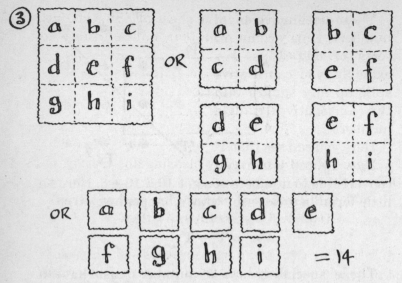

If your sheet has 3 × 3 stamps ... there's one big 3 × 3 square, four possible 2 × 2 squares and nine single squares: 1 + 4 + 9 = 14 ways.

So far we've got the numbers 1–5–14 in our sequence. Does this sound familiar? It should do because the formula for the number of squares you can tear from a grid of n × n stamps is the same as the nth square pyramid number!

Here's a little trick question that will catch your friends out: how many squares are there on a chess board with 8 × 8 squares? *And the answer is not 64! Think about all the square patterns that measure 2 × 2 and 3 × 3, etc.*

Answer: a chess board measures 8 × 8 squares, so the total number of possible squares you can find is the eighth square pyramid number which is 204.

If you have a rectangular sheet of $f \times g$ stamps, how many ways can you tear out a square *or* rectangle shape?

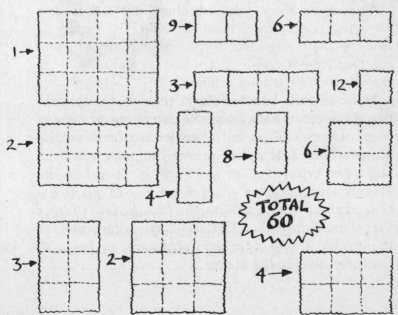

Here's one of those really pleasing answers:

★ Total number of rectangles and squares from a $f \times g$ rectangle = $T_f \times T_g$

It's the two triangle numbers of the sides multiplied together! Let's try it out with a sheet that has 3 stamps along one side and 4 on the other. First we'll make all the different shapes and see how many of each one we can get:

Now we'll try the formula which says we should get $T_3 \times T_4$ which is $6 \times 10 = 60$ squares and rectangles. It works!

Alien interpreters

Don't panic, but word has reached us that the evil Gollarks from the planet Zog are planning to invade Earth. Of course, this is quite a regular thing, but this time it seems the Gollarks are serious. To boost their chances, they have decided to join up with the Intergalactic Ploog Warriors.

There's just one small problem. The Gollarks can't speak Ploog and the Ploogs can't speak Gollark, so they need an interpreter who can speak Ploog and Gollark.

So far so good, but then they decide that they could use some extra help from the Avenging Mabels of Mopbukket. This is a tad awkward because the Mabels have a completely new language that the other two types of alien can't speak. Therefore the Mabels need *two* extra interpreters, one to talk to the Gollarks and one to talk to the Ploogs. Don't forget that there is already a Gollark–Ploog interpreter, so that makes a total of three interpreters, as shown by the three lines in the diagram.

Now the fourth type of alien turns up. It's the Tods of Yom who only speak Toddish. Let's see what happens with our diagram…

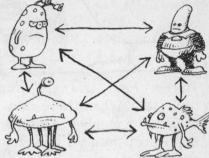

The six lines represent six interpreters. Next we'll add the Bolshides…

… and then the Rutters …

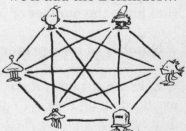

Now look back at all the diagrams and see how the number of interpreters is changing: 1–3–6–10–15 … it's the triangle numbers that we saw back on page 17! How very exciting.

Here's how triangle numbers fit in with interpreters. When there were four alien languages involved, the number of interpreters needed was the *third* triangle number (which is 6). When there were five languages, the number of interpreters needed was the *fourth* triangle number (which is 10). So if there were L different languages to deal with, you just subtract 1 from L to find the triangle number that gives the number of interpreters needed.

★ **Number of interpreters for L languages = $T_{(L-1)}$**

Let's try our formula to see how many interpreters are needed for TWENTY types of aliens all speaking different languages! As $L = 20$ and the number of interpreters we need is $T_{(L-1)}$ this tells us that we need to work out T_{19} which is the nineteenth triangle number. Therefore we use the triangle number formula but replace n with 19.

Number of interpreters needed =

$$T_{19} = \frac{19(19 + 1)}{2} = \frac{19 \times 20}{2} = 190$$

Wow! Twenty different lots of aliens need 190 interpreters.

HAH! WE'VE GOT 47 DIFFERENT ALIEN RACES ALL SET TO INVADE EARTH AND THEY ARE SENDING 10 WARRIORS EACH!

So THAT'S 470 ALIEN WARRIORS COMING TO GET YOU!

Er...my pyjamas are in the lawnmower...

Or is it 'The wet cushion is angry'?

Don't panic. 470 alien warriors would be scary ... but let's use our formula to see how many interpreters they need! Here L = 47 so we need the 46th triangle number.

$$T_{46} = \frac{46(46 + 1)}{2} = \frac{46 \times 47}{2} = 1081$$

Yahoo! They have more than twice as many interpreters as warriors, so it should be cosy aboard their spacecrafts. Let's watch them setting off...

Oh well, at least that's one way to get everyone talking the same language.

The pizza formula

The Pure Mathematicians spend a lot of time arguing over the best pizza formula.

Luckily there is one pizza formula they can agree on, but it has nothing to do with the toppings. Instead it involves chopping the pizza up into separate bits, and it makes a nice puzzle that you can try for yourself.

Imagine you've got a HUGE round pizza and a very long straight knife. Before you touch the pizza, you've got one BIG bit. Now if you do a single long cut right across the pizza, how many bits do you get? (The answer is 2.)

Now do another long cut across the pizza. You get 4 bits.

Now do a third cut ... what is the *biggest* number of pieces you can make? (The pieces do NOT have to be the same size or the same shape.) The answer is not 6 or 8 ... it's 7! And if you do a fourth cut the biggest number of pieces you can make is 11. If you don't believe it, then count them:

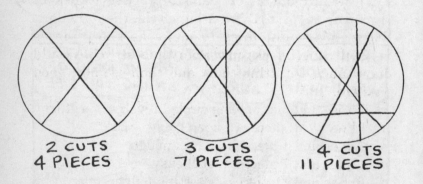

2 CUTS
4 PIECES

3 CUTS
7 PIECES

4 CUTS
11 PIECES

What is the biggest number you can make with five or even six cuts?

So far we've started with one whole pizza, then got 2 bits, then 4 bits then 7 then 11 bits. 1–2–4–7–11 doesn't make a pattern we've seen but what happens if we subtract 1 from every number? We get 0–1–3–6–10 ... yes it's the triangle numbers again! So if we just add 1 to the triangle number formula we get this essential piece of mathematical delight:

★ The maximum pieces of pizza formula
$$= \frac{c(c + 1)}{2} + 1$$

where c = the number of cuts

So if you cut the pizza 7 times you could get:

$$\frac{7(7 + 1)}{2} + 1 = \frac{56}{2} + 1 = 28 + 1 = 29 \text{ pieces}$$

Now to be honest, to get 29 pieces with 7 cuts needs a very big pizza and a very sharp knife, especially if the cheese is all gluey. It also takes a LOT of skill, but if you want to practise there's an easy way to do it. Draw a big circle, then divide it up with straight lines to make as many pieces as you can. Check how many pieces you should have made with this chart and then see how good you are.

- 0 lines and just one big circle ... well, it's a start
- 1 line and 2 pieces ... keep going
- 2 lines and 4 pieces ... easy enough
- 3 lines and 7 pieces ... still easy
- 4 lines and 11 pieces ... getting tougher
- 5 lines and 16 pieces ... very good
- 6 lines and 22 pieces ... amazing skill
- 7 lines and 29 pieces ... truly fantastic
- 8 lines and 37 pieces ... we don't believe you

Hint: each time you draw a line, it must cross all the other lines, but not at a point where two lines already cross each other.

Had fun? Well that's all going to stop now because nice round circular pizzas are EASY.

The Crescent Pizza Formula
City: **Chicago, Illinois, USA**
Place: **Luigi's Diner, Upper Main St**
Date: **17 November 1928**
Time: **8:30 pm**

The blinds were down, the heat was up, the lights were low and the tension was high in Luigi's Diner. Seven shady men sat around the central table staring at what was on the plate in front of them. Six were angry and one was dabbing his mouth with a chequered napkin, clearly embarrassed.

"I didn't know it was for sharing!" mumbled Porky Boccelli, trying not to go crimson with embarrassment.

"We just had enough money for one pizza between the seven of us," snapped the Weasel. "And you've taken over half of it with one bite!"

"Look at it," moaned Chainsaw Charlie. "It looks like one of those, whad'ya call the things ... like a yellow moon shape."

"A crescent," said Numbers, the thinnest man.

"That's right!" nodded the others.

"Nah," said Chainsaw. "I meant banana. It looks like a fat pointed banana."

"Well whatever it looks like, my little brother's had his share," said Blade Boccelli. "So I guess we divide the rest up between six of us."

"We won't be getting much each," muttered Half-smile Gabrianni. He turned towards the waiter who was standing on the next table, reaching up and scraping dead flies off a light bulb. "Hey Benni, what ya doin' with your bare feet on the table?"

"This is a posh place," explained Benni. "We try to keep it nice for you guys. You want me to put my muddy shoes where you eat?"

"Guess not," said Half-smile. "But when you're finished, can you fetch us a knife?"

Just then there was a draught from across the room. A cold voice said, "Leave it, Benni. We'll cut it for them."

A small bejewelled woman and a long grey man were standing in the open doorway. Immediately Blade and the others rose to their feet and backed away.

"Ma Butcher!" said Blade. "And Long Jake, what a surprise."

The long grey man's long grey lips curled upwards slightly at the edges. He enjoyed surprising people, but his surprises were never the nice sort.

"So Blade," said the woman, stepping towards the table and eyeing the remains of the pizza. "How's business? Things must be pretty good if you can afford to leave the table without finishing Luigi's house special. Mind if I take it for my dog?"

There was a tuneful chorus of seven hungry stomach rumbles, but none of the men dared object. Nobody ever dared object to anything when Long Jake was sliding a needle dagger from his sleeve.

"No, no!" muttered Blade. "You take it! Be our guest."

The woman laughed a laugh that sounded like a champagne glass hitting a steel door.

"Well that is kind!" she said. "Because I thought I heard you were planning to divide it between six of you. Is that right, Benni?"

"Er, yes ma'am, but maybe no ma'am, but I don't know ma'am," said Benni looking from one group to the other and wondering what was the best thing to say without upsetting anybody.

"I'll tell you what," said Ma Butcher. "Let's have some fun here. I say that Long Jake can divide your piece of pizza into six pieces with two straight cuts of his knife."

The men gasped. Surely it was impossible? But then if anybody could do anything with a knife, it was Long Jake.

"If Jake can't do it, I'll buy you all you can eat," said Ma Butcher. "But if he can do it, then Mr Snuffles gets your pizza for his din-dins. What d'ya say?"

"It's impossible!" muttered One-finger Jimmy. "Six pieces with two cuts?"

"So do we accept?" said Blade.

"Of course we accept," said Porky. "What's to lose?"

"You ain't got nothing to lose!" sneered the Weasel. "Because you had yours already!"

So is it possible to cut a crescent shape into six pieces with two straight cuts?

Shapes like squares or circles are called "convex". This means that if you were standing on a side looking outwards, you could not see any other part of the shape. However, shapes like crescents are called "concave". If you stood inside the curve of the crescent you could look across and see some more of the crescent shape. It's easy to remember which way round these words are...

HE CAN'T SEE HER SO HE'S VEXED

HOLLOW SHAPE A BIT LIKE A CAVE

If you draw a straight line across a convex shape such as a circle, you can only divide it into two bits, but if you draw a straight line across a concave shape like a crescent, you can make *three* bits!

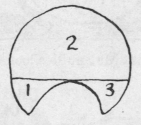

If you draw more straight lines, you can make even bigger numbers, and there's a formula for cutting crescents:

★ The maximum pieces of a crescent formula

$$= \frac{c(c + 3)}{2} + 1$$

where c = number of cuts

If Long Jake cuts the crescent twice, this should give a maximum of:

$$\frac{2(2 + 3)}{2} + 1 = \frac{2 \times 5}{2} + 1 = \frac{10}{2} + 1 = 5 + 1 = 6$$

… and here's what it looks like!

And here's what Mr Snuffles looks like:

Chopping in three dimensions

As we've seen, if you cut across a circular pizza 3 times you can get a maximum of 7 different bits. However if you have a lump of cheese the size of a washing machine and cut it 3 times, you can get 8 bits! This is because you can cut it horizontally as well as vertically.

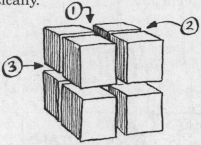

Here's a formula that's vital for picnics:

★ **Maximum number of pieces of cheese you can get with n cuts**

$$= \frac{n^3 + 5n}{6} + 1$$

ON THE MOVE

The Road Test

Once again those brave boys and girls of the Murderous Maths research department are pushing back the frontiers of knowledge by investigating the formulas for speed. We'll see how our Pure Mathematicians are getting on soon, but first we'll look at the basic speed formula which is very simple: **distance = speed × time** which we can write as $d = st$. There are three different versions of this depending on what you want to work out:

$$\star\ d = st \qquad s = \frac{d}{t} \qquad t = \frac{d}{s}$$

This is how each one works:

$d = st$

If you know your speed and how long you've been moving, then you can work out how far you've travelled.

Before we can work out how far the Colonel has travelled, the first thing is to make sure the units all match up. The problem is that his speed is 4 metres *per second* and he's been going for 10 *minutes*. The easiest thing to do here is to convert the 10 minutes into seconds. As there are 60 seconds in each minute, the time = 60 × 10 = 600 seconds. Now we can use $d = st$ by making $s = 4$ and $t = 600$. We get $d = 4 \times 600$ = 2,400 metres.

$$s = \frac{d}{t}$$

If you know the distance you have travelled and how long it's taken you, then you can work out what speed you've been doing. This is especially entertaining in the summer if you're in a car trying to get to the seaside.

To work out your speed you just divide the distance by the time. You get 2 miles ÷ 4 hours and so you can happily announce:

$$t = \frac{d}{s}$$

If you know the distance and speed, you can work out the time. This is the formula that the Pure Mathematicians are using in their first experiment to calculate exactly when and where the police will catch them. To make the sums simpler, they are measuring their speeds in metres per second. This means "metres divided by seconds" so it usually gets written as m/s or even ms^{-1} (because anything to the power of −1 means you divide by it).

The Pure Mathematicians know that the police are travelling 5 ms^{-1} faster than they are and they also know that the police have to catch up 500 m. Therefore they can use $t = \frac{d}{s}$ to work out the time it will take the police to catch them up. $d = 500$ and $s = 5$ so $t = 500 \div 5 = 100$ seconds.

Now they know that the time is 100 seconds, they can also work out how far they will travel before the police catch them by using $d = st$. Their speed is 20 ms^{-1} and the time is 100 seconds therefore the distance will be $20 \times 100 = 2{,}000$ metres.

Of course, the research hasn't quite finished yet. The Mathsmobile is now parked outside the police station next to the police car and one of our heroes is inside, kindly helping the police with their enquiries.

This is a bit more complicated to work out, but the clue is that both the police and the Mathsmobile are setting off from the police station, and once the police have caught up, they will stop at the same place. Therefore they will both travel the same distance so we'll see what we can do with the $d = st$ formula.

First we'll try and make some sort of equation for the police. We don't know the real speeds, so we'll just call the police speed S. We don't know the times either, so we'll just call the time it takes for the police to catch up T. We'll call the distance they travel before they catch the Mathsmobile D. If we put these together we get an equation for the police which is $D = ST$. This obviously hasn't got us very far yet, but be patient...

Now we'll see what happens for the Mathsmobile. We know it travels at $\frac{9}{10}$ of the police speed so the Mathsmobile speed is $S \times \frac{9}{10}$. We also know the Mathsmobile started 15 seconds earlier, so when the police finally catch them the Mathsmobile will have been travelling for $(T + 15)$ seconds. The distance they travel is the same D so we can put an equation for the Mathsmobile:

$$D = S \times \tfrac{9}{10} \times (T + 15)$$

As we already know $D = ST$ we can substitute the D and put:

$$ST = S \times \tfrac{9}{10} \times (T + 15)$$

At this point we are allowed to get slightly excited because both sides of the equation are multiplied by S.

The rules of algebra say we can divide both sides of an equation by anything we like except zero. Obviously S can't be zero otherwise everybody's speed would be 0 and nobody would be going anywhere. Therefore let's divide both sides by S:

$$T = \tfrac{9}{10} \times (T + 15)$$

Multiply both sides by 10 $\qquad 10T = 9 \times (T + 15)$

Multiply out the bracket $\qquad 10T = 9T + 135$

Subtract $9T$ from both sides $\qquad T = 135$

Remember that T is the time for the police, and $(T + 15)$ is the time for the Mathsmobile. So has the formula worked?

So thanks to our dedicated team of Pure Mathematicians, we have proved that the formulas $t = \frac{d}{s}$ and $d = st$ both work. There's just the $s = \frac{d}{t}$ formula to try now...

45

Acceleration

Things are fairly simple when you're just toddling along at a steady speed, but the real fun starts when you speed up or slow down. Getting faster is called *acceleration* and getting slower is usually called *deceleration*.

The odd thing is that speed is measured in *metres per second* (written as ms^{-1}) but acceleration is in *metres per second per second* which can be written as ms^{-2}. We can explain this with a simple experiment. All you need is:

- a mountain of ice
- a polythene suit
- washing-up liquid
- a speedometer
- a stopwatch

First you need to build a slide down the side of your ice mountain. Next you put on your polythene suit and smear it all over with washing-up liquid. It's worth it because when you come down the slide there will hardly be any friction to slow you down. (We could have suggested that you do this experiment on the moon where there won't be any air resistance either, but we didn't want to make things too complicated.)

Climb to the top of the slide and get ready with your stopwatch and speedometer. Before you start your speed is 0 ms^{-1}. Start your stopwatch and give yourself a little push off...

46

If you keep an eye on the time that's passed and the speed you're going, here's what you might see...

When you first set off you go quite slowly, but as each second passes your speed steadily increases from 0 to 3 to 6 to 9 ... ms^{-1}. Therefore for every second you travel your speed is increasing by 3 metres per second which means your acceleration is 3 metres per second *per second* or 3 ms^{-2}.

The formula for acceleration (if you're not moving when you start) is:

$$\star\ a = \frac{s}{t}$$

a = the acceleration
s = your final speed
t = the time you've been accelerating

After the first second you were going at 3 ms^{-1} therefore $s = 3$ and $t = 1$ and so $a = 3$.

If it takes you 20 seconds before you hit the bottom, how fast will you be going at the end?

We jiggle around the speed/acceleration formula to give:

$$\star\ s = at$$

By the time you finish we know that $a = 3$ ms^{-2} and $t = 20$ seconds. Therefore your final speed would be $3 \times 20 = 60$ metres per second which is quite fast. (It's 216 km per hour or about 135 miles per hour.)

How far will you have travelled down the slide? For this we use the distance/acceleration formula where d = the final distance travelled:

$$\star\ d = \frac{1}{2}\,at^2$$

We know a = 3 ms^{-2} and t = 20 so we get $d = \frac{1}{2} \times 3 \times 20^2 = 600$.

So your slide was 600 metres long.

How to make a big BOOM

Get two Mount Everests and put one on top of the other to make a giant mountain about 17,700 m high. Cover them with ice and make a steep slide at an angle of about 65° to the ground. (Your slide will end up being about 19,500 metres long.) Cover your polythene suit with LOADS of washing-up liquid to make the friction tiny, and if possible put your giant mountain in a vacuum chamber so that there's no air resistance. Done that? Good.

Set off from the top. If your acceleration is 3 ms^{-2} how long will it take to reach the bottom?

If we fiddle around with the distance/acceleration formula we get:

$$\star\ t = \sqrt{\frac{2d}{a}}$$

Put in d = 19,500 and a = 3 to get $t = \sqrt{\frac{2 \times 19{,}500}{3}} = \sqrt{13{,}000}$ = about 114. Therefore it will take you about 114 seconds to reach the bottom. How fast will you be going in the end? Use $s = at$ to get

$s = 3 \times 114 = 342$. Your speed will be about 342 ms^{-1}.

Here's the good bit! Anybody watching you will hear a massive BOOM as you reach the end, because you'll have crashed through the sound barrier. (Sound travels at about 340 ms^{-1}.)

How to speed up

The speed/acceleration formula $s = at$ assumes that you're not moving before you start. However if you're already moving before you accelerate you need a slight adjustment to the formula:

$$\star \; s_2 = s_1 + at$$

s_2 = your final speed
s_1 = the speed you were already going
a = acceleration
t = the amount of time you're accelerating.

Let's imagine you're in a dustbin that's already rolling along the road at 10 ms^{-1}.

You hit a slope that accelerates you at 2 ms^{-2} for 7 seconds. How fast will you end up going?

$s_2 = 10 + (2 \times 7) = 10 + 14 = 24$ ms^{-1}.

If you want to find out how far you travelled while speeding up you need a formula that allows for the fact that you were already moving.

$$\star\; d = s_1 t + \tfrac{1}{2}at^2$$

s_1 is your speed before you started accelerating so that was 10 ms^{-1}. We also know that $a = 2$ ms^{-2} and $t = 7$ so we get:

$d = 10 \times 7 + \tfrac{1}{2} \times 2 \times 7^2$

Here's where it's vital to do the bits in the right order (see page 15). There's no brackets, so do the powers first. You get $d = 10 \times 7 + \tfrac{1}{2} \times 2 \times 49$. Next you do the multiplying to get $d = 70 + 49$, and finally do the adding to get $d = 119$ metres.

How to slow down

Slowing down is usually called deceleration which is the same as negative acceleration. Suppose you're still in your dustbin going at 24 ms^{-1} but you roll through a patch of wet tar for 5 seconds.

If the tar makes you decelerate at 3ms^{-2} what will your final speed be?

We can use $s_2 = s_1 + at$ again, but this time remember that the acceleration is negative so $a = -3$. We know $s_1 = 24$ and $t = 5$ so we get $s_2 = 24 + (-3 \times 5) = 24 - 15 = 9$. Therefore your new speed will be $9\ \text{ms}^{-1}$.

Stopping time

One of the most important calculations involved with speed, time, distance and acceleration is how much time it takes you to stop.

Here we've got a massive ocean liner toddling along at a majestic $6\ \text{ms}^{-1}$. One of the problems with liners is that they are very big and heavy and they don't have very good brakes. Even with the propellers in reverse and everybody standing on the front blowing as hard as they can, the maximum deceleration might only be 0·02 ms⁻². How many seconds will it take to stop?

If you start with the $s_2 = s_1 + at$ formula, you can turn it into $t = \frac{s_2 - s_1}{a}$. However s_2 is the final speed so that's just zero. You end up with $-s_1$ on the top, but bear in mind that as you're slowing down, a will also be negative so the two negatives cancel out. We get:

$$\star \textbf{ stopping time } t = \frac{s}{a}$$

s = original speed
a = deceleration

With our ocean liner $s = 6$ and $a = 0·02$ therefore $t = 6 \div 0·02 = 300$ seconds. That's *five minutes*!

Stopping distance

What's even more important to know than stopping time is how far you'll travel before you stop. This is especially true when there's an ocean liner advancing on an upturned dustbin with somebody in it. If we combine the $d = \frac{1}{2}at^2$ and $t = \frac{s}{a}$ formulas we get $d = \frac{1}{2} \times a \times (s/a)^2$ which nicely boils down to...

$$\star \textbf{ stopping distance } d = \frac{s^2}{2a}$$

s = original speed
a = deceleration

For our liner we put in $s = 6$ and $a = 0·02$ and get $d = \frac{6^2}{2 \times 0·02} = 900$ m.

It takes 900 metres before the liner comes to a stop!

The scary part of this formula is that the original speed is squared. Suppose our liner was going twice as fast, i.e. $s = 12$ ms^{-1}? You might think it would take twice as far to stop but actually if you work out $\frac{12^2}{2 \times 0.02}$ you find it will travel 3,600 metres before it comes to a halt. This is *four* times the distance!

Therefore if you're driving your ocean liner across the bay and see an ice-cream van parked on the pier, ask yourself three very important questions before you steer towards it.

People who drive cars are always being warned that if they go just a little bit faster, they need a much longer stopping distance in an emergency. In fact this formula explains that a car travelling at 40 miles per hour takes almost twice as far to stop as a car travelling at 30 mph.

The drop zone

About 400 years ago the Italian genius Galileo did an experiment which involved dropping a cannonball and an egg from a high building. When they hit the ground at the same time, he realized that things falling to earth all accelerate at exactly the same speed. It doesn't matter how heavy they are. (The only thing that makes a difference is air resistance. If you drop a brick and a piece of tissue paper, the brick will hit the ground first. But if there was no air, they would hit the ground at the same time.)

If they had been using metres in those days, Galileo could have found out another neat result. When you drop an egg from a high building, after 1 second it will be going at 10 ms^{-1}, after 2 seconds it will be going at 20ms^{-1} and after 3 seconds it will be going at 30ms^{-1} ... so the acceleration caused by gravity is 10 ms^{-2}.

OK, we'll admit it. The acceleration due to gravity isn't *exactly* 10ms^{-2}. At sea level it's more like $9 \cdot 81 \text{ ms}^{-2}$ and up mountains it gets slightly less. However there are so many painful numbers in physics that when the number 10 crawls onto your lap in a friendly fashion, you give it a stroke behind the ears and a saucer of milk without asking awkward questions.

In formulas the acceleration due to gravity is usually represented by a little *g*. So if you don't know what a *g* is for, it probably means 10 (or $9 \cdot 81$ if you're being fussy).

If you drop a hippopotamus out of an aeroplane, how far will it fall in 5 seconds? Remember g is the same for everything including hippopotamusesseses so we use $d = \frac{1}{2}at^2$ putting in $a = 10$ and $t = 5$. We get $d = \frac{1}{2} \times 10 \times 5^2 = 5 \times 25 = 125$ metres. But hippos falling out of planes is a bit dull so here's a bit more fun...

You're a pigeon sitting on top of the Eiffel Tower in Paris and you see a massive hat approaching from the Champs-Elysées. You can't resist a bit of target practice. If the tower is 300m high, how long before you hear someone shout something like "Zut alors"?

You can rearrange the $d = \frac{1}{2}at^2$ formula to show that the time it takes something without a parachute or wings to fall to the ground is:

★ **dropping time** $= t = \sqrt{\dfrac{2h}{g}}$

t = time in seconds
h = height you dropped it from
g = acceleration due to gravity

For our pigeon's experiment $h = 300$ m and $g = 10$ ms^{-2} (that's close enough for pigeons) so we fill these into the formula and get: $t = \sqrt{\frac{2 \times 300}{10}} = \sqrt{60} = 7{\cdot}75$ seconds.

We haven't been able to check this sum ourselves but maybe there's a French pigeon Murderous Maths reader who'd like to test it for us and let us know. Merci beaucoup.

Cannons

Urgum the Axeman is trying out his brand new Bombastic Decimator cannon, and of course being a true barbarian, he hasn't bothered to check the instructions.

$V = 70 \, ms^{-1}$

If he fires his cannon straight upwards, how high will the cannonball go? To work it out you need to know v, the *muzzle velocity* of the cannon which is how fast the ball is moving when it shoots out of the end. (You also need to ignore air resistance, or the sums get too murderous even for a Murderous Maths book.)

Let's say the muzzle velocity v of the cannonball is $70 \, ms^{-1}$. As the ball flies up in the air gravity will be reducing the speed by $10 \, ms^{-2}$. When the ball comes to a stop it will have reached its maximum height.

We can get a special formula for the maximum height just by changing the letters in the stopping distance formula: $d = \frac{s^2}{2a}$. The stopping distance d becomes the maximum height h, s = the velocity v and a = gravity acceleration g so we get:

$$\star \text{ maximum height} = h = \frac{v^2}{2g}$$

g is 10 ms^{-2} and v = 70 ms^{-1} so we get: h = $\frac{70^2}{2 \times 10}$ = 4900 ÷ 20 = 245 metres.

Just for fun, we can find out how long it takes the cannonball to get up there by putting $s = v$ and $a = g$ into the stopping time formula $t = \frac{s}{a}$.

★ **time to reach maximum height** = $\frac{v}{g}$

So Urgum's cannonball stops going up after 70 ÷ 10 = 7 seconds. What happens next?

Yes, it comes down again. The curious thing is that the drop zone formula will tell us how long it takes to fall: $t = \sqrt{\frac{2h}{g}}$. But we already know $h = \frac{v^2}{2g}$ so look what happens when we swap h in this formula for $\frac{v^2}{2g}$. We get:

Time to fall to the ground again $= \sqrt{\frac{2}{g} \times \frac{v^2}{2g}} = \sqrt{\frac{2v^2}{2g^2}} = \sqrt{\frac{v^2}{g^2}} = \frac{v}{g}$

In case you hadn't noticed, the time to reach the maximum height and the time to fall down again are both $\frac{v}{g}$. Because these times are the same, this leads to another neat result. Once your cannonball starts falling, it accelerates at g which is 10 ms⁻². We know the time it takes to fall is $\frac{v}{g}$ therefore how fast is it going when it hits Urgum's foot? We use $s = at$ and get the speed to be $g \times \frac{v}{g} = v$. Yes, the cannonball hit Urgum's foot at exactly the same speed as it left the cannon!

Urgum is going to have to think of a cunning way to fire his cannon without hitting his foot, but there's no rush. He's got until the end of the book.

A useless fact

No human being has ever jumped up and been in the air longer than 2 seconds.

Of course this doesn't count things like jumping off cliffs or wearing a rocket jet pack or reverse bungee jumps.

We can prove this by thinking about the world record for the high jump which is about 2·5 metres. So how long would you be in the air if you did manage to jump 2·5 metres?

As we saw with the cannonball, it takes the same time to go up as it does to come down, so if we work out how long it takes to fall 2·5 metres and double it, that's the time you'd be in the air. We'll use the drop zone formula: $t = \sqrt{\frac{2h}{g}}$. h = 2·5 and g = 10 so we get $t = \sqrt{\frac{2 \times 2 \cdot 5}{10}} = \sqrt{\frac{5}{10}} = 0 \cdot 707$ seconds.

So the maximum time to go up AND down is 2 × 0·707 = 1·414 seconds.

In fact if you wanted to stay in the air for 2 seconds, you would need to jump to a height of ... *5 metres*!

CAN YOU FEEL THE FORCE?

Back in the 1680s the genius Isaac Newton explained what force is and how it works in his massive book known as the "Principia". The book was 550 pages long and basically it said that nothing starts moving or changes direction unless you give it a shove. "Ho ho," you laugh because it all seems so obvious now, but it's a bit more complicated than that. If you're on a roller coaster that's zooming around and spinning you upside down, it's not really the speed that's exciting. What gives you the real buzz are the forces you can feel pushing on you to make you go faster, slow down, change direction and end up with your breakfast all over your shoes.

Isaac had to do tons of tricky sums to work out exactly what was happening with force. You might have heard the story of an apple whacking him on the head and giving him ideas, but the truth is that he got a lot of his results from seeing how the sun, moon and planets move round. It's just a pity that he wasn't around long enough to feel the forces on a roller coaster.

Here comes one of the amazing formulas that helped him.

The speed of planets

In 1609 a German astronomer called Johannes Kepler published this neat formula:

$$\star \frac{T^2}{d^3} = k$$

T = the time taken for a planet to go round the sun
d = the average distance of the planet from the sun
(Don't worry about k because it disappears in a minute.)

If we didn't know how far away Mars is from the sun we could use this formula to work it out. First of all we need another planet that we know about, so we'll use Earth. We know that the time for Earth to go round the sun = 1 year and we know that the distance of Earth from the sun = 150 million km.

We can put these numbers into Kepler's formula: $\frac{1^2}{150^3} = k$.

The next job is to see how long it takes Mars to go round the sun so grab your stopwatch.

THERE IT IS!

TIKKA TIKKA TINK

IT'S TAKEN 1·88 YEARS.

Let's call the distance from Mars to the sun m and put it with the time of 1·88 years into Kepler's formula: $\frac{1·88^2}{m^3} = k$.

Here's the good bit! As both versions of the equations
= k, we can get rid of the k and
get this: $\frac{1^2}{150^3} = \frac{1\cdot88^2}{m^3}$

Shuffle everything round to get: $m^3 = 1\cdot88^2 \times 150^3$

Now we bash the numbers out: $m^3 = 11,928,600$

And then do the cube roots
and get: $m = 228$ (roughly)

So we've worked out Mars is about 228 million km
from the sun. And it is!

Not only did this equation help people find out
about the planets, it was one of the key clues that
helped Isaac Newton sort out...

Gravity

Back in the 1660s the story goes that Isaac was
sitting under an apple tree and an apple fell on his
head. He realized that the apple was attracted to the
Earth, and then went on to realize that absolutely
everything is attracted to absolutely everything else
according to this formula.

$$\bigstar\ F = G\frac{m_1 m_2}{d^2}$$

F = the force of attraction (in "newtons")

m_1 = the mass of the first object (in kilograms)

m_2 = the mass of the second object (in kilograms)

d = the distance between them (in metres)

G = the "gravitational constant" which is
0·0000000000667. (There are 10 zeros between
the point and the 667.)

The unbelievable part of this is that if everything is attracted to everything else, then even Pongo McWhiffy and Veronica Gumfloss should be attracted together.

You can pick any two objects you like, such as Pongo and Veronica, and the equation tells you the amount of force that's pulling them together. So let's say m_1 is Pongo who has a mass of 60 kg and m_2 is Veronica who has a mass of 50 kg and the distance between them is 1 metre. We can work out the force pulling them together:

$F = 0.0000000000667 \times 60 \times 50 \div 1^2 = 0.0000002001$ newtons

So does this mean that gravity is going to drag Veronica into Pongo's arms in a frantic moment of passion?

Our next formula will sort this out.

Newton's Second Law of Motion

★ *F = ma* or force = mass × acceleration

This formula is probably Isaac Newton's most famous discovery because it explains exactly what "force" does. Suppose you have an 8 kg lump of rock floating in space and you want to get it moving. You give it a steady push so that after 1 second the rock is moving at 5 ms⁻¹. This means that in one second the speed has increased from 0 ms⁻¹ to 5 ms⁻¹ so the acceleration is 5 ms⁻². (Acceleration was explained on page 46).

If you kept pushing with the same force, after 2 seconds your rock would be going at 10 ms⁻¹ and after 3 secs it would be going at 15 ms⁻¹. Although the speed is getting higher the acceleration is still 5 ms⁻².

The force needed to make a 1 kg mass accelerate at 1 ms⁻² is called **1 newton** after Isaac. So how much force would it take to make your 8 kg lump of rock accelerate at 5 ms⁻²? $m = 8$ and $a = 5$ so using the formula $F = ma$ the force = 8 × 5 = 40 newtons.

Although Isaac's equation is *almost* perfect, about 250 years later Albert Einstein realized that the rules change a bit when you're travelling near the speed of light. Here's his version of the equation:

★ Einstein's force formula $F = \dfrac{ma}{(1 - \frac{v^2}{c^2})^{\frac{3}{2}}}$

v = your velocity (or speed)
c = the speed of light which is 300,000 km per second.

As you can imagine, sums with this equation are quite murderous, but unless your speed is getting up towards 100,000 kilometres per second, you can stick to good old $F = ma$. Besides, when you're going at that sort of speed, time will be collapsing around you and your mass will be approaching infinity, so you'll have more to worry about than just a few sums.

In the meantime, remember Pongo and Veronica sitting on the park bench? We worked out that the force pulling them together is 0·0000002001 newtons so if Pongo was floating in free space, we could work out his acceleration towards Veronica.

WHOOPEE!

If we start with $F = ma$ we can swap it round to make $a = \frac{F}{m}$. The force is 0·0000002001 newtons and Pongo's mass is 60 kg, therefore Pongo is accelerating towards Veronica at 0·0000002001 ÷ 60 = 0·000000003335 ms^{-2}.

What's more, if Veronica was floating in free space instead of clinging on to her end of the bench, she would also be accelerating towards Pongo!

As Veronica's mass = 50 kg we use $a = \frac{F}{m}$ as before and find that Veronica is accelerating at 0·0000002001 ÷ 50 = 0·000000004002 ms^{-2}. This is bad news for Veronica! Because her mass is less, this means she is moving towards Pongo faster than he is moving towards her.

If we add these two accelerations together, we find that they are accelerating towards each other at 0.000000007337 ms^{-2}.

We can use the acceleration/distance equation $d = \frac{1}{2}at^2$ from page 49 to see how much closer they would be after one hour. The first thing is to convert the hour into seconds because all our other times are in seconds. As there are 60 minutes in an hour and 60 seconds in a minute, 1 hour $= 60 \times 60 = 3,600$ seconds. So $t = 3600$ and $a = 0.000000007337$ ms^{-2}.

$d = \frac{1}{2} \times 0.000000007337 \times 3600^2 = 0.04754$ metres.

In other words, if they were both floating in free space, after one hour they would be less than *5 centimetres* closer together. Mind you, as the distance between them gets smaller, the attractive force between them steadily increases, and so their acceleration builds up and they will move faster and faster and faster...

Pendulums

A "pendulum" can be any weight hanging down from a thin rod or a string and being allowed to swing freely. The amazing thing is that so long as it isn't swinging too far, the time (T) it takes to swing across and back again only depends on how long the pendulum is. It doesn't matter how heavy the weight is!

$$\star \; T \text{ (in seconds)} = 2\pi\sqrt{\tfrac{l}{g}}$$

l = the length of the pendulum

g = is gravity acceleration (as seen on page 55).

So if you take one of your shoes off and tie it to 1 metre of string and let it swing gently, the time taken for each complete swing backwards and forwards:

$$2\pi\sqrt{\tfrac{l}{g}} = 2\pi\sqrt{\tfrac{1}{9 \cdot 81}} = 2 \times 3 \cdot 1416 \times 0 \cdot 3193 = 2 \cdot 0065$$
seconds

You'll notice we made $g = 9 \cdot 81$ instead of 10 because we usually want to calculate time as accurately as possible. If you go up a high mountain g gets slightly smaller. If you use $g = 9 \cdot 6$ then your shoe would take $2 \cdot 028$ seconds to do a full swing which is slightly longer.

Einstein's energy equation

A chapter about force and mass and things moving would not be complete without the most famous formula of the twentieth century...

$$\star\ E = MC^2$$

As well as messing about with $F = ma$ Albert Einstein came up with this beauty. Albert realized that everything is made up of MEGA amounts of energy and if you completely destroy it, then the energy is released. (This is the sort of thing that happens in nuclear power stations.) E is the energy you get, M is the mass that you are destroying and C is the speed of light.

This is one scary equation so we'll move on quickly.

MONEY!

Making lots and lots of money is really easy and anybody can do it. All you need to do is follow the Murderous Maths two-step system:

Step 1   Buy something. (The money you pay is called the *cost price*.)

Step 2   Sell it for more money than you paid for it. (The money you get is called the *sale price.)*

What could be simpler?

How to calculate the greatness of your new wealth

The extra money you make is called *profit* and there's a simple formula to link sale price (s), cost price (c) and profit (p):

$$\star\ p = s - c$$

Of course you can jiggle it round to get $s = c + p$ or $c = s - p$. Once you've got the hang of cost, sale and profit then you're all ready for the cut and thrust of the unforgiving commercial world. So keep your wits about you as we visit...

The inhabitants of Fogsworth Manor have all been trying to raise funds for a new bird bath by clearing out their cupboards ... or in one person's case, clearing out somebody else's cupboard.

As you can see, Rodney Bounder has bought the trousers for £8, but now he hopes to make a profit by selling them for £12. It's easy to work out his profit. You start with $p = s - c$ and when you put the numbers in you get $p = £12 - £8$ so obviously Rodney's profit will be £4. All very simple so far, but here's the clever bit:

I ALWAYS TRY TO MAKE A PROFIT OF 50%

Profit margins and percentages

When you are buying and selling a lot of different items, it is far more use to describe the *profit margin* which is given as a fraction or even a percentage.

Percentages are a type of fraction. "Per cent" means "divide by 100" so if you have 9·5% that's the same as 9·5 ÷ 100 = 0·095.

People get quite confused with profits, prices and percentages, so before we go on, it's important to know which bit is which.

Cost price (c) The cost price is always the original price of the item before anything happens. (Remember this because it becomes very important later on.)

Sale price (s) The sale price is how much is paid for the item.

Profit (p) The profit is the difference in money

between the cost price and the sale price. Be careful though! If the cost price is more than the sale price, then the profit will be negative – in other words it's a loss!

Profit margin % (m) The profit margin is a fraction describing the profit as a percentage of the cost price. Eeek! Actually it's not so difficult as you'll see.

The big secret to combining cost, profit and profit margins in percentages is all wrapped up in this little formula:

$$\star \text{ Profit margin in \%} = m = \frac{p}{c} \times 100$$

Let's check Rodney's profit margin on the trousers. The cost price was £8 and the profit was £4. If we plonk c = £8 and p = £4 into the formula we get: $m = \frac{4}{8} \times 100$ which works out to $m = 50$. Therefore the profit margin is 50%. Rodney has charged the right amount for the trousers!

All the profit and percentage formulas you'll ever need...

As well as the profit margin formula, we've also seen that $s = c + p$ and if you know about algebra then you can fiddle these around to work out any cost, sale, profit or profit margin percentage. However this isn't really meant to be an algebra book, this is a formulas book and so Murderous Maths is now proud to present every variation on these formulas you might need. So long as you know the values of two of the letters c, s, p, or m you can work out any of the others.

73

$$\star\ s = c + p \qquad = c\left(\frac{100 + m}{100}\right) \qquad = p\left(\frac{m + 100}{m}\right)$$

$$\star\ c = s - p \qquad = \frac{100p}{m} \qquad = \frac{100s}{100 + m}$$

$$\star\ p = s - p \qquad = c\left(\frac{m}{100}\right) \qquad = s\left(\frac{m}{100 + m}\right)$$

$$\star\ m = \frac{p}{c} \times 100 = \frac{p}{s - p} \times 100 = \frac{s - c}{c} \times 100$$

Let's see how to use these formulas. What else has Rodney got for sale?

The vase is priced at £6 and we know he hopes to make 50% profit, so how much did he pay for it to start with? (By the way, have a guess first. Do you think the answer is £3 or £4?)

The first thing is to decide which formula we need. We want to work out c which is the cost price that Rodney paid. We know $s = 6$ and $m = 50$ so look along the line of formulas that begins with $c =$ to find the one that has s and m in it. We find that $c = \frac{100s}{100 + m}$ so when we put the numbers in we get $c = \frac{600}{150} = £4$.

We've done it! Rodney's cost price for the vase was £4.

(Be honest – did you think it was £3? This is a mistake that just about everybody makes. But if Rodney bought the vase for £3 and sold it for £6, then his profit would have been £6 – £3 =£3. Using the $m = \frac{p}{c} \times 100$ formula we can see that $m = \frac{3}{3} \times 100$ which tells us that his profit margin would have been 100%!)

Let's see what else Rodney is up to.

What should he write on the price tag?

First we'll try it without a formula. As Rodney's profit is 50% of £3 it will be £1.50. We just add his profit to the £3 he paid to find that the price on the tag should be £4.50. That was simple enough but if the numbers had been more awkward it would have been easier to use a formula, so let's see what to do.

We want to work out s. As we know $m = 50\%$ and $c =$ £3, we'll put them into the $s = c\left(\frac{100 + m}{m}\right)$ formula and get:
$s = 3\left(\frac{100 + 50}{100}\right) = 3\left(\frac{150}{100}\right) = 3 \times 1{\cdot}5 = £4.50$.

Good grief! We know that Rodney's profit margin is 50%, but how much profit in real money did he make? We know $s = £7.50$ and $m = 50$ and we'd like to know p so we'll use $p = s\left(\frac{m}{100+m}\right)$. When we put in the numbers we get:

$p = £7.50 \times \left(\frac{50}{100+50}\right) = £7.50 \times \left(\frac{50}{150}\right) = £7.50 \times \frac{1}{3} = £2.50$.

Rodney is clearly having a very good afternoon, but the trouble is that not *everybody* makes a profit...

Coping with loss

Binky bought the trousers for £12 but is selling them at £9, so what is his profit?

We know c = £12 and s = £9, therefore if we use $p = s - c$ we find that his profit is £9 – £12 = –£3. The negative sign means that he is going to make a loss! What's more if you use the $m = \left(\frac{s-c}{c}\right) \times 100$ formula you'll find his profit margin will be –25%.

It's very important to get the negatives in the right place. Earlier on Binky bought up a selection of amusingly carved vegetables.

Sadly during the heat of the afternoon they turned into a shrivelled mush and he sold them to Auntie Crystal at a loss of 60%.

So how much did Auntie Crystal pay for them?

His profit p was –£3 his profit margin m was –60%, and we want to know the sale price s. We use $s = p\left(\frac{m + 100}{m}\right)$ and make sure we put all the negatives in! We get $s = -£3 \times \left(\frac{-60 + 100}{-60}\right) = -£3 \times \left(\frac{40}{-60}\right) = -£3 \times -\frac{2}{3} = £2$.

Auntie Crystal paid £2, but most importantly all the negatives cancelled out. That was lucky for Binky, because if Auntie Crystal had paid him *minus* £2 then that would have meant he would have paid her for taking the vegetables away!

Poor old Binky. Everybody seems to be packing up and going away, and he's *still* stuck with a pair of trousers that nobody wants...

78

Special offers

Have you ever seen signs in shops that say things like *"20% off"* or *"All Prices Down 30%"*? This means that they are offering you a *discount* which means you pay less money. You can use the formulas we've seen to keep track of everything so long as you remember that from the shop's point of view discount is the same as making a loss. Therefore p and m will be negative.

c is the original price of the item.

s is the sale price (i.e. how much you have to pay)

p is the amount of money the original price has been reduced by, so it is negative!

m is the discount percentage and it is also negative because it is making the original price smaller.

How much should you pay for the TV? We know the original price (or the *cost* price) is £200. We also know the discount percentage m is −15%. We need to know the sale price s so we can use $s = c\left(\frac{100 + m}{100}\right)$. When we put in the numbers we get $s = £200 \times \left(\frac{100 - 15}{100}\right) = £200 \times \left(\frac{85}{100}\right) = £200 \times 0.85 = £170$.

How much money did he save?

Be careful – it's tempting to think that the amount saved is 40% of the price he paid (i.e. £90 $\times \frac{40}{100}$ = £36), but it's not! It's 40% of the original cost. We know s and m and we want p so let's grab the $p = s\left(\frac{m}{100 + m}\right)$ formula. $s = £90$ and remember that m is a discount percentage so it's negative: $m = -40$. We get $p = £90 \times \left(\frac{-40}{100 - 40}\right) = £90 \times \left(\frac{-40}{60}\right) = -£60$.

So the "profit" is −£60 which means the amount saved is £60.

Chocolate bargains

Sometimes in shops, instead of saying prices are lower, they might say you get extra of something. In our formulas m is always a percentage, but the letters c, s and p don't have to represent money. You can also use them for measurements such as litres of lemonade, metres of rope or even grammes of...

CHOCOLATE!

If the original chocolate box had 500 grammes of chocolate in it, how much will the new one have?

The original size is 500 g which is c because in our formulas c represents the original. m is +35 (this time it's positive because the size has got bigger) and we need to work out s because that represents the value after the orginal has been adjusted. The formula to use is $s = c\left(\frac{100 + m}{100}\right)$. If we take our time and carefully work out the answer we find that the new box contains exactly...

... well it *did* contain 675 g.

Interest

If you're really rich you might want to put your money into a bank or building society. If you do, this makes all the people who work behind the counter very happy because when the bank is closed they like to play with it. Sometimes they spread all the money out on the floor and roll on it, other times they have money fights where they scoop it up into big bundles and throw it at each other. They also like to see how much cash they can shove up their cardigans or stuff down their trousers, or if they're feeling really naughty, they fold the biggest notes into paper darts and see if they can throw them right across the room and into the shredder. (By the way, have you ever noticed that banks always have signs and blinds blocking the view from the windows? That means whenever the bank is closed, you can never see inside. Now you know why.)

The bank people are so glad to have your money that they pay you for lending it to them. The more money you let them have, the more they pay you and the extra amount you get is called *interest*. The amount of interest you earn is worked out by the *interest rate*. There are various ways of working out interest and each has its own formula.

Simple interest

A simple sort of interest rate is 5% p.a. The letters p.a. stand for "per annum" which is Latin for "per year", so this means that you get an extra 5% of the amount you've paid in added on every year. Although interest rates are nearly always given as percentages, interest sums are much easier if you convert the

percentage to a decimal fraction. Remember that %
means "divide by 100" so 5% means $\frac{5}{100}$ or 0·05.

Suppose you put in £600 and the interest is 5% p.a.,
what extra money would you get after three years?

★ Interest = $p \times t \times r$

p = your premium (in other words how much
money you put in the bank).

t = time in years

r = interest rate per year (as a decimal fraction)

We put $r = 0·05$, $t = 3$ and p = £600 into the formula
and find that after three years the extra money you'd
get = £600 × 3 × 0·05 which comes to £90.

How much money would you have in total? You
could add your £600 to the £90 interest to give £690,
but this formula does it automatically for you:

★ Total money with interest = $p(1 + t \times r)$

Dear Lucky Person,
Your long-lost great Uncle Biggles died 12
years ago and put £1,500 in a savings
account for you at an interest rate of
6·5% p.a.
Yours jealously,

Comp and Sayshun (solicitors)

Good old Uncle Biggles! Let's use the formula to see
how much money is waiting for you. p = 1,500 and t =
12. We need to make r into a decimal so we do this: 6·5%
= $\frac{6·5}{100}$ = 0·065. Now we put the numbers in the formula:

Total money = £1,500(1 + 12 × 0·065)

HINT: remember to do the bit inside the brackets first, starting with multiplying / dividing.

Total = £1,500(1 + 0·78) = £1,500(1·78) = £2,670

The £1,500 Uncle Biggles left you has turned into £2,670 thanks to a bit of interest!

One thing you should know about these simple interest accounts: the bank people usually only add the interest once a year on a fixed date, e.g. June 30th. If you put your money in the week before (e.g. June 23rd), then they don't count it as a full year, they would only count it as one week which is $\frac{1}{52}$ of a year. So if you put in £100 on June 23rd and the interest rate is 4% p.a. then on June 30th they will work out that you have £100(1 + $\frac{1}{52}$ × 0·04) which comes to £100 and about 8 pence.

Compound interest ... and MORE money!
Wasn't it good that the bank turned Uncle Biggles's £1,500 into £2,670 after 12 years?

Actually they should give you more than that.

Unfortunately Uncle Biggles put the money into Binky's bank who are all terribly decent chaps but sadly they can only work out simple interest. In other words each year they only paid you 6·5% interest on the £1500 that Uncle Biggles put in, so each year you got exactly £1,500 × 6·5% = £97.50. After 12 years they had given you 12 × £97.50 = £1,170 interest.

But that's a bit unfair!

After the first year they gave you £97.50 so during the second year you didn't just have £1,500 in the bank, you had £1,597.50. In the second year, instead of just getting interest on the £1,500, you should also be getting interest on the extra £97.50 – in other words you should be getting *interest on your interest*! In the third year, not only do you want interest on the interest for the first year, but you also want interest on the interest from the second year which came from the interest on the first year! And if the money is there for 12 years you want interest on the interest on the interest on the interest ... you get the general idea.

All this interest on interest is called *compound interest,* it's much fairer and is what most banks would give you. Here's how the first few years would look:

		Compound interest	Total savings
Cash put in =	£1,500		£1,500
Interest for the first year =	£1,500 × 6.5% =	£97.50	
Total after first year =	£1,500 + £97.50 =		£1,597.50
Interest for the second year =	£1,597.50 × 6.5% =	£103.84	
Total after second year =	£1,597.50 + £103.84 =		£1,701.34
Interest for the third year =	£1,701.34 × 6.5% =	£110.59	
Total after third year =	£1,701.34 + £110.59 =		£1,811.93

By now you'll be desperate to know how much Uncle Biggles' £1,500 would have been worth after 12 years of compound interest at 6·5%, so thank goodness there's a special formula for it:

★ Total savings (with compounded interest)
$$= p(1 + r)^t$$

We know p = £1,500, r = 6·5% and t = 12 so let's put them in:

Total = £1,500$(1 + 0·065)^{12}$
    = £1,500$(1·065)^{12}$
    = £1,500 × 2·129
    = £3,193.64

Good grief! If Uncle Biggles had put the money in a compound interest account instead of Binky's you'd have £3,193.64 instead of £2,670. Even though the little bits of interest on the interest don't seem much, when you put them all together over 12 years they make an extra £523.64.

It makes you wonder what Binky's bank could have been doing with all that extra money they should have given you, doesn't it?

Exponential interest ... and EVEN MORE money!

Suppose you got a postal order for £1,000,000 for your birthday and you put it in the bank, and the interest rate was 7% p.a. After a year, the interest you'd expect would be 7% of £1,000,000 which is £70,000.

Actually they should give you more than that.

You have only been given 7% interest on your £1,000,000. This isn't fair because the £70,000 interest isn't earned all at once in a big bouncy lump at the end of the year, it gradually builds up over the 12 months. As there are 365 days in the year, the interest rate for the first day is $7\% \times \frac{1}{365} = 0.019178\%$. This might not look much, but if you have £1,000,000 then after the first day you should have made an extra £191.78. This £191.78 is your money and it sits in the bank for another 364 days until the end of the year, so you should get some interest on that too!

Therefore on the second day you get 0·019178% interest on your £1,000,000 *plus* you should get 0·019178% interest on your £191.78 which comes out to about $3\frac{1}{2}$p. On the third day you get interest on your £1,000,000 plus interest on the £191.78, plus interest on your $3\frac{1}{2}$p. It's time we had a diagram.

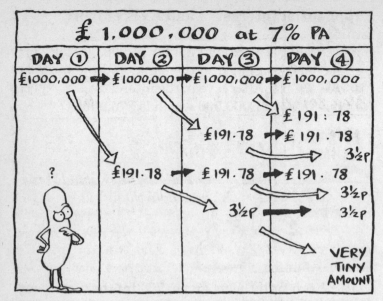

Under each day is the total amount of money you have in the bank. You'll see each bit of money has two arrows coming from it. The black arrows show the money is still there the next day and the white arrows show the new interest that's arrived.

The only difference to what you get with normal interest is the little amounts of $3\frac{1}{2}$p that get added in. When you've got £1,000,000 that doesn't sound like much, but it's worth thinking about. On day three the first $3\frac{1}{2}$p arrived. On day four two more lots of $3\frac{1}{2}$p arrived (and there's also the $3\frac{1}{2}$p that was there before, making three × $3\frac{1}{2}$p in total). On day five, three more lots of $3\frac{1}{2}$p will arrive, on day six, four more lots will arrive … and at the end of the year on day 365 then 363 extra lots of $3\frac{1}{2}$p will have turned up.

Here's a diagram to show how the $3\frac{1}{2}$ps build up. (Ignore the mystery line for now).

DAY	3	4	5	6	7	8		365
NUMBER OF EXTRA 3½Ps	1	2	3	4	5	6 …		363
TOTAL OF 3½Ps SO FAR	1	3	6	10	15	21…		66066
MYSTERY LINE!	0	1	4	10	20	35…		

ADD

Look at the "total of 3½ps so far" line. It goes 1–3–6–10 ... would you believe it's the triangle numbers AGAIN! (see page 17). We can use the triangle numbers formula to see how many extra 3½ps we'll have by the end of the year. It's the 363rd triangle number so:

$$T_{363} = \frac{363 \times 364}{2} = 66,066$$

Yowee! By the end of the year we have 66,066 extra lots of 3½p which is £2,312.31.

Actually they should give you more than that.

When we worked out the interest on £191.78 in a day to be 3½p, that was only an approximation. The real answer was 3·678p and 66,066 lots of 3·678p is £2,429.91 which is over £100 more! Sometimes it's worth calculating tiny fractions of a penny.

You'll notice back in our "Exponential Interest" diagram we didn't bother working out the "very tiny amount" of interest you'd get on 3·678p every day. (It comes to 0·000705p). The first tiny amount appeared on day four. So how many tiny amounts should we have on day five? There are three $3\frac{1}{2}$ps in the bank on day four, so each of those give us a tiny amount of interest on day five, plus we still have the one tiny amount we already got on day four. That means on day five we finish with $3 + 1 = 4$ tiny amounts of interest.

Now have a look at the "mystery line" of our table. This represents the tiny amounts of interest building up. You'll see days four and five have the numbers 1 and 4. Day six has 10 tiny amounts and the arrows show they come from the 4 tiny amounts we already had on day five plus an extra tiny amount of interest for each $3\frac{1}{2}$p we had on day five. In fact as we go along the mystery line we are adding up the triangle numbers, and this makes *tetrahedral* numbers (see page 19)! As the tiny amounts of interest don't start until day four, the total number of tiny amounts for the year is the 362nd tetrahedral number. Here's where we use the tetrahedral formula:

The nth tetrahedral number = $\dfrac{n^3 + 3n^2 + 2n}{6}$

So we just casually swap n for 362 and get:

Number of tiny amounts of interest:

$$= \frac{362^3 + 3 \times 362^2 + 2 \times 362}{6} = 7,971,964$$

So you multiply this by 0·000705p and find the interest on the interest on the interest comes to £56.20.

So how much money can we expect at the end of the year?

There's our original money	£1,000,000
There's the interest on the original	£70,000
The interest on the interest	£2,312.31
And the interest on the interest on the interest	£56.20
Total =	£1,072,368.51

Not bad eh?

Actually they should give you EVEN more than that.

Of course we could work out the interest on the interest on the interest on the interest ... but when you've got £1,000,000 in the bank you probably can't be bothered to add up the first 361 tetrahedral numbers and multiply the answer by the interest on 0·000705p each day (which is 0·0000001352p).

The thing to think about is what *time* did you put your money into the bank? If you're making over £190 a day in interest, then in the first hour you'll make £7.90. Surely by the second hour you'll want interest on your new £7.90?

Maybe you should update your account every minute ... or *every second*?

Relax. There is an answer to all your worries.

Sound the trumpets and throw a party for a pert little formula that allows for interest on interest on interest on interest for every tiniest fraction of a second right through the whole year. And in case you wonder how a formula can be "pert"...

★ Total cash in the bank = pe^{rt}

p = your premium (how much money you put in the bank to start with).
t = number of years
r = interest rate (as a decimal fraction)
e = 2·718281828459...

The clever bit is the letter e which is used to represent that rather odd number. (The decimal fraction goes on for ever but we couldn't be bothered to print any more of it.) The posh description of e is "the base of natural logarithms" which doesn't mean much to most of us. In fact e helps to deal with anything that grows faster when it gets bigger and that includes your £1,000,000. On the first day you got £191.78 more, but the next day you got £191.81$\frac{1}{2}$ more, so your money grew faster. You can use e to get an idea of what's happening with plants and animals too because every part of every living thing grows all the time, therefore the bigger they get, the faster they grow. There's a bit more about e in *Numbers: the Key to the Universe*, but for the meantime we'll use the formula to see what happens to our £1,000,000 in a year with interest of 7%.

p = £1,000,000
r = 0·07
t = 1

Total = £1,000,000 × $2{\cdot}7182818^{0{\cdot}07 \times 1}$

If you don't want to do this in your head, you'll need a calculator with an e^x button. To work out $2{\cdot}7182818^{0{\cdot}07}$ you just push e^x and then 0·07 and you get 1·072508181. All you do now is work out £1,000,000 × 1·072508181 and get:

Total = £1,072,508.81

The total we got to on page 91 was £ 1,072,368.51, but if we had worked out *all* the interests of interests of interests ... *and* done the sums for every billionth of a second right through the year, then we would have got an extra £140.30.

How do banks get rich?
Although banks love having your money, occasionally they find themselves having to lend some out to people. However they have a system for making themselves more money which is so simple it's brilliant.

When you let them have your money, they pay you a *low* interest rate.

When they lend you some money they charge a *high* interest rate.

For instance if Gertrude puts £100 in, they might give her 5% interest but if Agatha borrows £100 they might charge her 7% interest, so basically we've gone right back to where this chapter started with $p = s - c$.

If Gertude puts in £100 and Agatha borrows £100 at the same time, the bank pays Gertrude £5 but it charges Agatha £7 so the profit $p = £7 - £5 = £2$. They've made £2 and it's cost them nothing.

As we said, it's simple but brilliant.

THE DAY OF THE WEEK ALGORITHM

Have you ever wondered what day of the week
- your granny was born on
- Christmas day will be in the year 2500
- it is *today*?

If you've ever tried to work out this sort of thing you'll find yourself facing the same problems as Pongo McWhiffy did as he tried to rekindle the fading memories of a distant romance…

Amazingly enough, there is a way to work out what day of the week any date falls on. You use a special *algorithm* which is a fancy name for a list of jobs you have to do. This algorithm involves sorting out a few mini-formulas and then it finishes with this weird beast:

★ **Day** =
$$(date + y + [\frac{31m}{12}] + [\frac{y}{4}] - [\frac{y}{100}] + [\frac{y}{400}])\text{MOD}7$$

What a beauty eh? You'll see where y and m come from and what the special [ ] brackets and MOD7 mean in a minute, but first here's a guide to which bits of the formula cope with the different problems.

96

30 or 31 days? The algorithm allows for the fact that the months April, June, September and November only have 30 days each, and the other months have 31 days except February. In the formula the $[\frac{31m}{12}]$ bit deals with this.

February 29th? This is the really awkward bit. February usually has 28 days except in leap years when it has 29 days. There's a letter f that turns up in the process which helps sort this out.

When are leap years? Leap years come every four years unless it's the start of a new century such as 1800 in which case there is NO leap year ... but if the year divides by 400 then it IS a leap year. (The year 2000 was a leap year but 2100 won't be.) This is all worked out by the $[\frac{y}{4}] - [\frac{y}{100}] + [\frac{y}{400}]$ bits.

If you thought that leap years caused trouble, the algorithm has an even bigger problem to deal with. It has to avoid creating any fractions or decimals. You'd look pretty silly if you discovered you were born on Monday·741 or $\frac{1}{2} \times$ Thursday. Therefore the algorithm uses two rather quaint maths tricks called INT and MOD.

INT means *integer division* which is a real treat for lazy people. An integer is a whole number, and when you do an integer division you only keep the whole number in the answer. The good bit is that you just throw away any remainders or fractions, you don't even bother rounding the answer up or down! We'll show where we need integer divisions by using square brackets like these: [ ].

If you work out $\frac{14}{5}$ the normal way you get 2·8. However if you work out $[\frac{14}{5}]$ you just get an answer of 2 because the [ ] brackets tell you to throw away the decimal fraction. What's especially important is this: $\frac{5}{8}$ would normally make 0·625 but $[\frac{5}{8}]$ = 0. We completely ignore the fraction and just get nothing!

Calculator tip:

Some calculators have an INT button − but if yours doesn't then all you need is a saw. Put in your dividing sum, e.g. $[\frac{47}{3}]$ would be 47 ÷ 3. You get the answer 15·6666... Now just saw through the calculator where the decimal point comes and throw the bit on the *right* right away, and then the correct answer will be left on the *left*.

MOD means *modulus* which is almost the opposite of INT. This time you do divisions but the only bit you're interested in is the remainder! So if you see (14)MOD5, this tells you to divide the 14 by 5 and get an answer of 2 with a remainder of 4. However the MOD bit means that you ignore the 2, it's just the 4 that matters! Therefore (14)MOD5 = 4.

Here's some others: (55)MOD6 = 1, (33)MOD20 = 13, (42)MOD8 = 0. This last one is true because when you do 42 ÷ 8 the answer is exactly 6 and there's no remainder.

The six steps of the algorithm

You start by working out a value for the letter *f,* and then use this to work out values for letters *m* and *y* which you can finally put into the big formula.

STEP 1   Pick numbers for the *date* (1–31), *month* (1–12) and *year* (e.g. 1994) you're working out.

STEP 2 $\quad f = [\dfrac{14 - month}{12}]$

This bit makes an adjustment depending on whether you've got past February or not. (If your month is January or February then f will come out as 1. Otherwise f will be 0. It can't be anything else.)

STEP 3 $\quad y = year - f$

Unless your date is in January or February, then y will be the same as the year.

STEP 4 $\quad m = month + 12f - 2$

STEP 5 $\quad$ Day =

$$(date + y + [\dfrac{31m}{12}] + [\dfrac{y}{4}] - [\dfrac{y}{100}] + [\dfrac{y}{400}]) \, \text{MOD} \, 7$$

Thanks to the MOD7, this formula will give you an answer of 0, 1, 2, 3, 4, 5 or 6.

STEP 6 $\quad$ Convert to the day of the week:

0 = SUNDAY
1 = MONDAY
2 = TUESDAY
3 = WEDNESDAY
4 = THURSDAY
5 = FRIDAY
6 = SATURDAY

Let's see if it works by testing it on a granny and seeing what day of the week she was born on. Her date of birth is the 19th of January 1931, so off we go.

STEP 1   date = 19, month = 1, year = 1931

STEP 2

$$f = [\frac{14 - month}{12}] = [\frac{14 - 1}{12}] = [\frac{13}{12}] = [1 \cdot 0833] = 1$$

STEP 3 $y = year - f = 1931 - 1 = 1930$

STEP 4 $m = month + 12f - 2 = 1 + (12 \times 1) - 2 = 11$

STEP 5   Day =

$$(date + y + [\frac{31m}{12}] + [\frac{y}{4}] - [\frac{y}{100}] + [\frac{y}{400}])\text{MOD}7$$

$$= (19 + 1930 + [\frac{31 \times 11}{12}] + [\frac{1930}{4}] - [\frac{1930}{100}]$$

$$+ [\frac{1930}{400}])\text{MOD}7$$

$= (19 + 1930 + [28 \cdot 42] + [482 \cdot 5] - [19 \cdot 3] + [4 \cdot 825]) \text{ MOD}7$

$= (19 + 1930 + 28 + 482 - 19 + 4)\text{MOD}7$

$= (2444)\text{MOD}7$

If you divide 2444 by 7 you get 349 and a remainder of 1. As MOD7 only wants the remainder, the final answer comes out as ... 1.

STEP 6   Check the list and you'll find the 19th of January 1931 comes out as a MONDAY.

We did this experiment with a real granny and the answer was right – she *was* born on a Monday!

If you want to find out what day Christmas 2500 is, then you put *date* = 25 *month* = 12 and *year* = 2500. When you go through the steps f is just 0 so $y = 2500$ and $m = 10$. Shove this into the big formula and get:

$$(25 + 2500 + [\frac{31 \times 10}{12}] + [\frac{2500}{4}] - [\frac{2500}{100}]$$

$$+ [\frac{2500}{400}])\text{MOD}7$$

$$= (25 + 2500 + 25 + 625 - 25 + 6)\text{MOD}7$$
$$= (3156)\text{MOD}7$$

$3156 \div 7 = 450$ with a remainder of 6 so that tells us that Christmas 2500 will be on a Saturday!

Warning!
If you're studying history, days of the week get a bit confused before the year 1753 because people were changing their calendar systems over and some days got missed out.

PERMS, COMS AND THE UNKNOWN FORMULA

In *Do You Feel Lucky?* there are all sorts of formulas that deal with permutations and combinations. Formula fans love them because they use the factorial sign "!" which means you multiply a number by all the numbers down to one, e.g. $4! = 4 \times 3 \times 2 \times 1 = 24$. The fun bit is that perms and coms produce circus tent-sized sums that look really scary, but they just cancel down and pop like bubbles when you start to work them out. Look at this:

$$\frac{8!}{3! \times 5!} = \frac{8 \times 7 \times 6 \times 5 \times 4 \times 3 \times 2 \times 1}{3 \times 2 \times 1 \times 5 \times 4 \times 3 \times 2 \times 1} = \frac{8 \times 7 \times 6}{3 \times 2 \times 1}$$

$$= \frac{8 \times 7 \times 6}{6} = 8 \times 7 = 56$$

POP!

Permutations – putting coins in order

Permutations means how many different ways you can line up a group of objects. It gives us one of the neatest formulas in the book:

★ **Permutations of *n* different objects = *n*!**

Dolly Snowlips has accused someone of loitering with an offensive face, so Lieutenant Ptchowsky has pulled in five of the usual suspects for an identification parade. How many different ways could the suspects be lined up? The answer is 5! (which is $5 \times 4 \times 3 \times 2 \times 1 = 120$)

$$= 5! = 120 \text{ WAYS}$$

Life gets more interesting when your objects are *not* all different. For instance if three of the Lieutenant's five suspects decide to wear identical clown masks, then it reduces the number of ways they can be arranged.

$$= \frac{5!}{3!} = 20 \text{ WAYS}$$

If all five suspects wore clown masks, there is only one way to arrange them.

$$= \frac{5!}{5!} = 1 \text{ WAY}$$

The easiest way to make a formula that deals with a mixture of objects is to divide the different objects into groups. Suppose Dolly now accuses somebody of grievous bodily odour, and the Lieutenant wants to line up 12 people. Five are wearing clown masks, two are wearing rabbit heads, three have giant shades and bald wigs on, and the last two forgot to disguise themselves so they look different.

GROUP a | GROUP b | GROUP c | GROUP d | GROUP e

★ **Permutations with repeats =**
$$\frac{\textit{Total number of objects}!}{(\textit{group a})! \times (\textit{group b})! \times (\textit{group c})! \times \dots}$$

We've got 12 suspects in total, and there are five in group a, two in group b, three in group c, one in group d and one in group e. When we put this into our formula we get $\frac{12!}{5! \times 2! \times 3! \times 1! \times 1!}$. As 1! just makes 1 this becomes $\frac{12!}{5! \times 2! \times 3!} = 332,640$ ways that the suspects could be lined up.

This seems like a big number, but bear in mind that if the Lieutenant pulls off all the disguises so that the suspects *all* look different then the total number of ways you could arrange them in a line is $12! = 479,001,600$.

Combinations: choosing cards and lottery numbers

You've got seven different playing cards, and you are allowed to choose any four of them. The set of cards you pick is called a *combination*. If the order of the cards matters then here's the formula to see the number of ways you can pick and arrange your cards:

★ **Combinations where order does matter** = $\dfrac{n!}{(n-p)!}$

n = total number of *different* items you can choose from

p = number of items you're allowed to choose

In this case $n = 7$ and $p = 4$, so the number of ways you can pick and arrange the cards = $\frac{7!}{(7-4)!} = \frac{7!}{3!} = 840$.

If the order matters then these two sets of cards would both count separately...

However with combinations, usually *the order does not matter*. (The two sets of cards above would only count as one combination because they both contain the same four cards.) This way you get fewer possible combinations and here's the more usual formula:

★ **Combinations where order does NOT matter**
$$= \dfrac{n!}{p!(n-p)!}$$

n = total number of *different* items you can choose from

p = number of items you're allowed to choose

So if you are choosing four cards from seven, the number of different ways you can do it is $\frac{7!}{4!(7-4)!}$ = $\frac{7!}{4! \times 3!}$ = 35.

Incidentally, there's a short cut to writing combinations. Instead of writing "how many ways can you choose p items from n different items in any order?" you can just put $_nC_p$. Here we just worked out that $_7C_4 = 35$.

One of the best known ways that combinations come up is when people choose their lottery numbers. In the UK people can pick 6 out of 49 different numbers (and the order does not matter), so the number of possible ways they can do it is $_{49}C_6$ which is $\frac{49!}{6! \times 43!}$ = 13,983,816. As only one of these combinations will win the jackpot, this means the chance of picking the winning combination is 1 in 13,983,816 which is approximately 1 chance in 14 million.

Combinations: throwing dice

When you're picking playing cards or lottery numbers, every card or number in your combination will be different. However things get very different when the same thing can turn up more than once, and this is what happens when you throw dice.

How many different combinations are possible with 4 dice? Each die has a "choice" of six numbers it can land on (so n = 6), and the four dice will end up choosing four numbers for you (so p = 4). If the order of the dice *does* matter then:

★ Repeated combinations when the order matters = n^p

In this case the number of possible results from 4 dice is $6^4 = 1,296$. But people hardly ever care about the order of dice, all that matters is the combination of numbers.

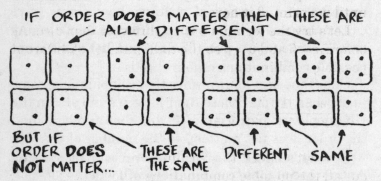

IF ORDER **DOES** MATTER THEN THESE ARE ALL DIFFERENT

BUT IF ORDER **DOES NOT** MATTER... THESE ARE THE SAME DIFFERENT SAME

So how many different combinations can we get from a set of dice when the order *doesn't* matter? The answer comes from a formula that has hardly ever been seen before! Get your camera ready because here comes...

The unknown formula

★ Repeated combinations when the order does NOT matter

$$= \frac{(p + n - 1)!}{p! \times (n - 1)!}$$

SPLIK

Did you take a picture? This is a very rare formula so take another one just to make sure, otherwise nobody will believe you actually saw it. The odd thing about this formula is that although it's quite useful and answers a reasonably simple question, it hardly appears in any other books or even on the internet. That's why it's almost completely unknown, or it was until we printed it here.

Let's try the formula out by throwing four dice. As before $n = 6$ and $p = 4$ so the total number of different possible combinations of four dice is:

$$\frac{(4 + 6 - 1)!}{4!(6 - 1)!} = \frac{9!}{4! \times 5!} = 126$$

Now let's check the formula's answer by writing out all the possible combinations of four dice.

1111 1112 1113 1114 1115 1116 1122 1123 1124 1125 1126 1133
1134 1135 1136 1144 1145 1146 1155 1156 1166 1222 1223 1224
1225 1226 1233 1234 1235 1236 1244 1245 1246 1255 1256 1266
1333 1334 1335 1336 1344 1345 1346 1355 1356 1366 1444 1445
1446 1455 1456 1466 1555 1556 1566 1666 2222 2223 2224 2225
2226 2233 2234 2235 2244 2245 2246 2255 2256 2266 2333 2334
2335 2336 2344 2345 2346 2355 2356 2366 2444 2445 2446 2455
2456 2466 2555 2556 2566 2666 3333 3334 3335 3336 3344 3345
3346 3355 3356 3366 3444 3445 3446 3455 3456 3466 3555 3556
3566 3666 4444 4445 4446 4455 4456 4466 4555 4556 4566 4666
5555 5556 5566 5666 6666

Although there are lots of other formulas that deal with dice combinations, the unknown formula can deal with *anything* that involves combinations where items can be repeated and the order does not matter. If you're not confused already then you soon will be because the Pure Mathematicians have been spotted in the paint shop.

111

If all six of the tins had to be different colours then the number of different shades the Pure Mathematicians could possibly make is $_8C_6 = 28$.

As the tins don't have to be different, (and the order they mix them up in doesn't matter), then the total number of possible shades they could make comes from the unknown formula. As they can choose

6 tins, then $p = 6$ and as there are 8 colours to choose from $n = 8$. Using the formula we get:

$$\frac{(6 + 8 - 1)!}{6! \times (8 - 1)!} = \frac{13!}{6! \times 7!} = 1,716 \text{ different possible shades}$$

Even though it's unknown, this formula has lots of different uses but unfortunately there's one thing that it can't do – it can't allow for taste. So here's a warning: if you don't want to see what three tins of pink paint, one of orange and two of silver look like all mixed up, then whatever you do avoid the Pure Mathematicians' bathroom.

ALL THE SHAPE AND LUMP FORMULAS YOU'LL PROBABLY NEVER NEED

It's decision time. What sort of person are you?

● A nice normal person.

If so, then you will have been quite satisfied with the neat list of shape and lump formulas back on page 10. Thank you.

● A Murderous Maths fan.

Is that what you are? Really? Then it goes without saying that the little list we've already seen wasn't enough for you, was it? Of course not, you need to know MORE. You're full of awkward questions such as....

We'd hate to leave you stranded so we've got three more thrill-packed chapters bursting with formulas. To ensure your maximum convenience and reading pleasure, here's how they've been divided up:

POLYGONALISH FORMULAS (PAGE 116)

This chapter tells you all you need to know about flat shapes with straight sides.

THAT'S FOR US!

BIZARRE BOXES (PAGE 143)

This one tells you all about any lumpy thing with straight sides.

YUP.

π FORMULAS (PAGE 150)

This chapter deals with any shape or lump with curved bits.

AT LAST! THE PERFECT SAUSAGE FORMULAS!

(Of course normal people are quite welcome to look at these chapters too, but be warned that you'll probably never ever need any of the formulas you find here ever. But there again, you never know...)

POLYGONALISH FORMULAS

A polygon is any shape made up of three or more straight lines and every single one of them produces a pile of different formulas for different things.

A guide to the letters we'll be using in this chapter

$a, b, c, d...$ **side lengths** – usually in little letters

$A, B, C, D...$ **angles** – usually in BIG letters

p **perimeter** – all the sides added together. It's handy for working out how long a fence you need to go round a cow field.

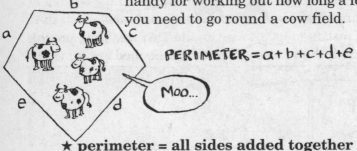

$$\text{PERIMETER} = a + b + c + d + e$$

MOO...

★ **perimeter = all sides added together**

s **semiperimeter** – which is half the perimeter. This is useless for working out how long a fence you need to go round a cow field because your cows will just wander off.

$$\text{SEMI-PERIMETER} = \tfrac{1}{2}(a + b + c + d + e)$$

MOO!

IT'S TIME WE MADE OUR MOOOOVE!

I FEEL LIKE STEVE McQUEEN ON HIS MOTORBIKE!

★ **semiperimeter** $= \frac{1}{2} \times$ **all sides added together**

You might think that semiperimeters are just pointless things to make life complicated, but they have a spooky habit of turning up in unexpected places. And after your cows have wandered off, they have a spooky habit of turning up in unexpected places too, so BEWARE.

R This is the **radius of the circumscribed circle** which is the smallest circle that can go round the outside of the shape. If you go for a curry at the Ravenous Rajah and sit at the biggest table (which is rectangular), Kumar has got a round table cloth that only just manages to cover the surface. This means the cloth is the size of the circumscribed circle.

With rectangles or squares, R is just $\frac{1}{2} \times$ the diagonal length so we get:

★ R (radius of circumscribed circle for rectangles)

$$= \frac{\sqrt{a^2 + b^2}}{2}$$

r This is the radius of the **inscribed circle** which is the biggest circle that can fit inside the shape. If you ask Kumar for the Beltsnapper Special, the plate it comes on is so big that it only just fits on the table without going over the edge. This is the size of the inscribed circle.

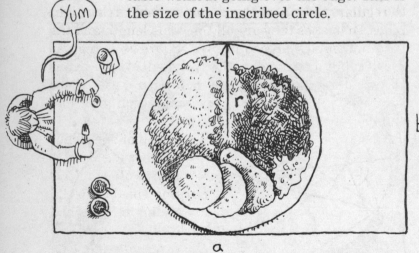

With rectangles there isn't much of a formula for r, it's just $\frac{1}{2} \times$ the shortest side. However if Kumar's table had been square and all the sides measured a, you get slightly neater results:

★ **Square diagonal = $a\sqrt{2}$ which means the same as $\sqrt{2} \times a$**

★ **R (radius of circumscribed circle for squares)**

$$= \frac{a}{\sqrt{2}}$$

★ **r (radius of inscribed circle for squares) = $\dfrac{a}{2}$**

It's time to leave the Ravenous Rajah now, so get your poppadom popped in and we'll move on.

Regular polygon formulas

A regular polygon can have any number of straight sides, so long as they are all the same length and the internal angles are equal. (A square is a regular polygon but a rectangle isn't.) Although Mr Reeve has drawn a regular five-sided pentagon here, these formulas will work for a regular polygon with *any* number of sides.

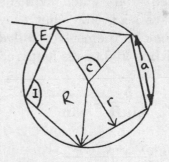

a = length of one side
n = number of sides
R = radius of circumscribed circle
r = radius of inscribed circle
E = external angle
I = internal angle
C = central angle

All you need to know is a and n, then you can use these formulas to work out anything else you want:

★ **central angle = external angle** $= \dfrac{360}{n}$

★ **internal angle** $= \dfrac{n-2}{n} \times 180$

★ **R (radius of circumscribed circle)**

$= \dfrac{a}{2 \times \sin(\frac{180}{n})}$

★ **r (radius of inscribed circle)** $= \dfrac{a}{2 \times \tan(\frac{180}{n})}$

★ **Area** $= \dfrac{na^2}{4\tan(\frac{180}{n})}$

Aha! You'll see that at long last we've got some trigonometry bits turning up (i.e. SIN and TAN). There's another one called COS which will be appearing soon. Trig bits are so groovy that they have already got a whole book to themselves called *The Fiendish Angletron* which is 208 pages long and includes such treats as:

★ **The SIN formula** $\dfrac{a}{\sin A} = \dfrac{b}{\sin B} = \dfrac{c}{\sin C}$

★ **The COS formula** $\cos A = \dfrac{b^2 + c^2 - a^2}{2bc}$

or $a^2 = b^2 + c^2 - 2bc\cos A$

However, for your convenience, we've gone through that book and crossed out everything that wasn't absolutely vital for working out formulas. By the time we'd finished, we'd got rid of $207\frac{1}{2}$ pages and now we've put the rest into this little box:

How to work out SIN, COS and TAN
You need a calculator with SIN COS TAN buttons on it. These functions convert angles into fractions. To work out SIN28° you push SIN 28 = and you should get something like 0·469.
If you see SIN⁻¹ COS⁻¹ or TAN⁻¹ then you have to do it the other way round, i.e. convert a fraction into an angle. This requires pushing the INV button. (Sometimes this is labelled as the SHIFT or even 2nd FUNCTION button.) So if you're working out TAN⁻¹0·82 you push INV TAN 0·82 = and you'd get 39·35°.

Formulas with SIN, COS and TAN are a bit spooky if you're not expecting them, but don't worry. You're more likely to see a pig with a powersaw than you are ever to need these trig bits, so you can relax. Sit back in your executive armchair, put your feet up on your executive desk and tinkle the little silver bell at your side which summons the servants to bring your executive fizzy pop and crisps.

You close your eyes and immediately you become swallowed up in a dream about solving polygon problems which is so lovely that you completely fail to hear the nasty banging and thumping noise coming from across the room. But even though your eyes and ears let you down, your nose takes a deep whiff of a foul brussel-sprouty smell and starts to panic. Your eyes open in surprise and you see a pig with a powersaw hacking at the doorway.

"Oh no!" you sigh when you realize what the smell is. It isn't the pig.

"Oh yes!" comes an evil voice. Curses! Your arch enemy Professor Fiendish steps into the room with a nasty leer on his face. "Har, har – expecting your pop and crisps were you? Well I've got a diabolical challenge for you, and unless you solve it, I'll tie a knot in your drinking straw so that when you try to use it, you'll have to suck so hard that your head will cave in."

How tremendously ghastly. Nevertheless you give him a cold stare as he steps aside to reveal that your doorway has been altered to a perfect octagon shape. A quick glance tells you that each of the eight sides measures precisely 0·7 metres.

"Well done, my trusty servant!" says the Professor patting his pet pig on the head. As he speaks, you notice he has swapped his nasty leer for a cunning leer. "All you have to do is work out the longest diagonal of your doorway," he leers cunningly.

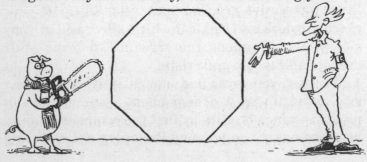

"Pah, simple!" you mutter. With deft precision you doodle an octagon and draw a perfect circumscribed circle around it. The radius of the circle is R and as the longest diagonal x goes right across the middle, obviously $x = 2 \times R$.

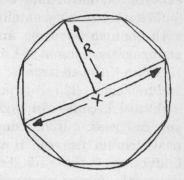

As we know that $R = \frac{a}{2 \times \sin(\frac{180}{8})}$, then we just multiply this by 2 to get:

★ The longest diagonal of a regular polygon with an EVEN number of sides =

$$\frac{a}{\sin(\frac{180}{n})}$$

It turns out that you'll have to use one of these SIN formulas after all, so here's what you do. You know $a = 0.7$ and $n = 8$ so you swap the letters for the numbers and get $\frac{0.7}{\sin(\frac{180}{8})}$. First work out the little bracket: $\frac{180}{8} = 22.5$. All you do now is grab your calculator and push in $0.7 \div$ SIN $22.5 =$ and you can tell the Professor the answer is 1.829 metres! Your drinking straw is safe.

"Sniffling sock juice!" mutters the Professor, and why shouldn't he? Just when he thought he'd got you, you beat him with a simple formula. But as you ponder this glorious thought, there's more banging afoot. Within seconds you see that the doorway has

123

now become a regular septagon! Each of the seven sides measures 0·7 m.

"What's the biggest diagonal now?" he sniggers with a triumphant leer. "And if you get this wrong, I'll stomp on your crisps so hard that you'll need to suck them up with the straw."

Oh dear. This looks awkward, because although you can work out R using the formula (it comes to 0·806 m), the longest diagonal x doesn't go across the middle of the circle, so it will be slightly *less* than $2R$. This makes things a bit more murderous, but luckily you've got one thing on your side that the Professor hasn't got. You've got FRIENDS!

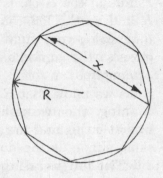

This is true. When this book was first being put together, the original formula we had to solve this problem was about the same size and shape of a combine harvester. Fortunately it was spotted by our formula consultants who ripped it to bits, and now thanks to the dynamic brains of Mr Kimpton and Mr Winch, we can now present you with this pocket-sized, power-packed, professor-popping formula:

★ **The longest diagonal of a regular polygon with an ODD number of sides =**

$$\frac{a}{2 \times \sin(\frac{90}{n})}$$

All you do is whack in $a = 0.7$ and $n = 7$ to get $\frac{0.7}{2 \times \sin(\frac{90}{7})}$. Put it into the washing machine, set it on "delicates" with a gentle spin cycle, hang it out on the line and then you can announce the answer...

1·573 METRES

In a ranting fury the Professor snatches the powersaw from the pig and with much cutting and cursing he transforms the doorway into an irregular tridecagon. Finally he stands back and puts his nasty, cunning, and triumphant leers all together on his face at once, unaware that his mouth is exactly the same shape as the doorway. All thirteen sides are different lengths and the angles are simply too ghastly to contemplate – and the doorway is just as bad.

"Have you quite finished?" you ask.

"Not quite!" he says, and with a deft whack of his hammer he smashes your calculator to bits. "Now see if you can work out what the longest diagonal of the doorway is! Har, har, HAR!"

About 10 seconds later...

"The longest diagonal is 1·67 metres," you say with confidence.

With a curse and a whimper the fiendish one turns his back and departs. He knows he cannot defeat your blazing brilliance. With a satisfied sigh you make a note of the formula you used to work out the diagonal:

Longest diagonal = Whatever it says on the ruler when you measure it.

After all, formulas are fun, but why make things hard for yourself?

Irregular polygons

There's only about one formula that's any use with irregular polygons:

★ **Total of internal angles = (n − 2) × 180°**

For Professor Fiendish's 13-sided doorway, the total of all the angles will be $(13 − 2) × 180° = 11 × 180° = 1,980°$.

If you want to work out the area of an irregular polygon then you usually need to split it up into triangles and work out the areas of all the triangles and add them up. So guess what's coming next...

Triangle area formulas

There are four main formulas to work out triangle areas: a simple one, two clever ones and a really fiddly one. (There's also a special bonus formula for

126

equilateral triangles.) First we'll check you know how the simple one works:

★ **Triangle area = $\frac{1}{2}$ base × perpendicular height**

Here we've got the base = 5 m and the perpendicular height = 4 m, so the area = $\frac{1}{2}$ × 4 × 5 = 10 m².

Life is especially easy if you have a right-angled triangle and you know the lengths of the two shorter sides, because if you treat one as the base, then the other will be the height. You get a really neat formula:

★ **Right-angled triangle area = $\frac{1}{2}$ × the two shorter sides multiplied together**

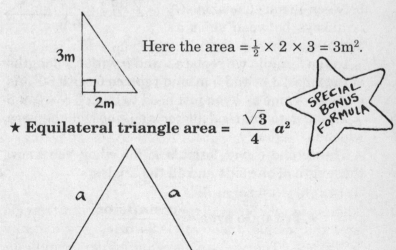

Here the area = $\frac{1}{2}$ × 2 × 3 = 3m².

SPECIAL BONUS FORMULA

★ **Equilateral triangle area = $\frac{\sqrt{3}}{4} a^2$**

So far so good, but if you don't know the perpendicular height of the triangle and it isn't equilateral then you have to use a cleverer formula. Clever triangle formulas are almost always based on this little diagram:

All you need to remember is that angle A is always opposite side a, B is opposite b and C is opposite c. Got that? Now you're ready for your first clever triangle formula:

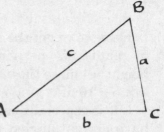

★ **Triangle area** = $\dfrac{1}{2} \times a \times b \times \sin C$ or $\dfrac{ab\sin C}{2}$

To use this formula you need to know the lengths of two sides and the angle between them. (The angle C is always between sides a and b.)

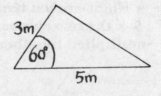

In the formula we replace a and b with the lengths of the sides, 3 m and 5 m, and replace C with 60°. As 0·5 is the same as $\frac{1}{2}$ you just need to bash 0·5 × 3 × 5 × SIN60° into your calculator and you get the area which is 6·495 m².

The second clever formula is for when you know the length of one side and all the angles.

★ **Triangle area** = $\dfrac{a^2\sin B\sin C}{2\sin A}$

Notice that the length you know is a and the angle A is the one opposite it.

The bad news: it isn't very pretty and you need to give your calculator a good bashing to get the answer. Here it is:

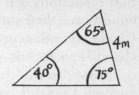

$$\frac{4^2 \times \sin65 \times \sin75}{2\sin40} = 10.895 \text{ m}^2$$

The good news: not many people know this one! If ever you're having a "who-knows-the-most-triangle-areas-formulas" competition, it could come in handy.

Finally it's time for one of the best things in this book. The fiddly formula works for any triangle, it doesn't need the perpendicular height and it doesn't need any angles. It just needs the three sides...

★ **Heron's semiperimeter formula for the area of a triangle =** $\sqrt{s(s-a)(s-b)(s-c)}$
where $s = \frac{1}{2}(a+b+c)$

You'll notice that the mysterious s which means the *semiperimeter* of the triangle has turned up! (And so has one of the cows. We warned you about that.) Remember that the semiperimeter is half of the perimeter, so that's the same as the three sides added together and then divided by 2.

It's now time to sit back for a minute and admire that formula. Even if you never ever use it (and be honest, you probably won't) – isn't it just fabulous? Obviously whoever thought up that beauty must have been a bit out of the ordinary, and if you look up the word "Heron" you won't be disappointed. You'll discover that this formula was invented by a big bird that stands in water eating fish.

Ho ho, we do like our jokes don't we? Actually the real inventor of this formula was one of the many clever people living in Alexandria about 2,000 years ago. Heron (or Hero as some people call him) had a nickname: it was "The Machine Man" because as well as doing some neat maths he invented enough entertaining gadgets to fill a gift catalogue. These included the first steam engine, a machine for firing arrows, a coin-operated drinks dispenser and lots of "automata" which are models of people and animals doing funny things. He even invented a spooky device for a temple. If you lit a fire in a big basin by the temple entrance, after a while the doors would swing open automatically, and when the fire went out the doors would slowly close.

To get the area of this triangle we first need s, the semi-perimeter. The perimeter is $7 + 8 + 9 = 24$ metres, so $s = \frac{1}{2} \times 24 = 12$ m. Now we swap a, b and c for the side lengths 7, 8 and 9 and plonk everything into the formula to get:

$$
\begin{aligned}
\text{Area} &= \sqrt{12(12 - 7)(12 - 8)(12 - 9)} \\
&= \sqrt{12(5)(4)(3)} \\
&= \sqrt{12 \times 5 \times 5 \times 4 \times 3} \\
&= \sqrt{720} \\
&= 26\cdot833 \text{ metres}
\end{aligned}
$$

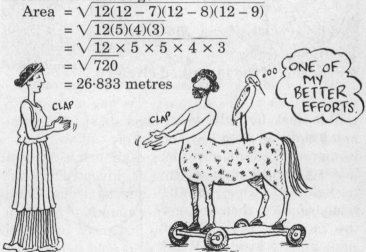

Incidentally, some people think that Archimedes might have known about this formula years before Heron ... but we don't think that Archimedes ever wrote it down. Maybe he just thought it was so obvious that he didn't bother.

Other triangle formulas

These are odd formulas that work for any triangle.

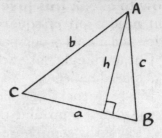

★ **Perpendicular height from side**
$a = b \times \text{SIN}C$ or
$c \times \text{SIN}B$

★ **R (radius of the circumscribed circle)** $= \dfrac{a}{2\sin A}$

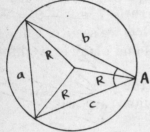

(In other words take any side, divide it by two and then divide it by the SIN of the opposite angle.)

★ **r (radius of the inscribed circle)** $= \dfrac{triangle\ area}{s}$

This last formula is so wonderful that even the cow is impressed. Think about it: if you know the area of *any* triangle, and divide it by the semiperimeter, then you get the radius of the smallest circle that fits inside it. Why? We don't know. We don't even want to know. We just think it's one of the wonders of the universe such as rainbows, homing pigeons, kebabs, Saturn's rings and wandering cows. We don't ask questions, we're just grateful that they are there.

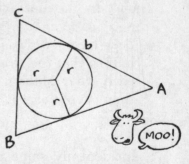

How to check this lovely formula really works

You need a bit of squared paper, some scissors, a ruler and a pair of compasses to draw a circle.

- Cut a triangle out of the piece of squared paper.
- Measure the three sides, add the lengths up and divide by 2 to get the semiperimeter.
- Count up all the squares on the paper as carefully as you can to work out the area. (E.g. if the squares measure 1 cm × 1 cm and you get 134·5 squares then the area will be 134·5 cm^2.)
- Divide the area by the semiperimeter to get the radius of the inscribed circle.

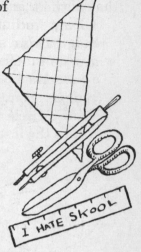

Now you've used the formula to work out the radius, you're going to make sure it's correct! To start with you need to **bisect** the angles of the triangle to find where the exact middle of the circle is. Here's the fun way of doing it:

- Take a corner of your triangle and fold it exactly in half so that the two sides of the triangle lie along each other. Make a crease right across the paper, then open it out.

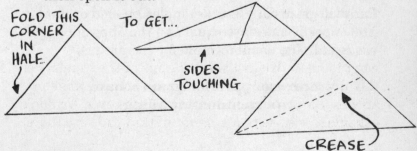

FOLD THIS CORNER IN HALF

TO GET...

SIDES TOUCHING

CREASE

- Fold another corner in the same way and open it out.
- And now for something slightly magical ... if you fold the third corner in the same way again, you should find all three creases cross at the same point! This should work for any shape of triangle.
- Set your compasses to the radius of the circle that you worked out with the formula, then put your compass point where the creases cross. When you draw a circle it should just touch all three sides! That's the inscribed circle.

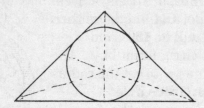

Parallelogram formulas

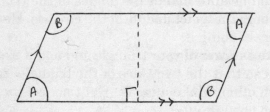

Parallelograms are like rectangles pushed over a bit. The opposite sides are equal and the opposite angles are equal. The usual formula for the area is:

★ **area of parallelogram = base × perpendicular height**

However, just like triangles, if you don't know the perpendicular height there's another much craftier formula for the area! You need to know the two different side lengths and *any* one of the angles.

**★ area of parallelogram = short side ×
long side × SIN(any angle)**

A parallelogram always has two matching angles that are bigger than the other two, but it doesn't matter whether you use a big angle or a small one, the formula works! This is because in parallelograms, one big angle and one small angle always add up to 180° and there's this odd little trig formula:

★ $\sin Z = \sin(180 - Z)$

Sadly semiperimeter cows are not allowed to wander across parallelogram formulas.

Rhombus formulas

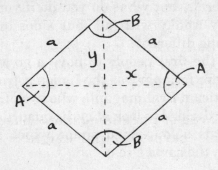

A rhombus is a square that's been pushed over to make a diamond shape. The sides are all the same length (we'll call them a), and this leads to two really neat area formulas. You can either use the parallelogram formula and get:

$$\star \textbf{ area of rhombus} = a^2 \times \text{SIN(any angle)}$$

OR if you happen to know the lengths of the diagonals x and y you get:

$$\star \textbf{ area of rhombus} = \tfrac{1}{2} \times x \times y$$

It's a lovely neat result, but again it's bad news for cows.

Wonky quadrilaterals

As you probably know, a quadrilateral is any shape with four straight sides. Squares, rectangles, parallelograms and rhombuses are all nice neat quadrilaterals, but what do you do if your shape is completely wonky with all four sides and all four angles being different?

One of the first people to have a go at getting a wonky shape formula was the Indian astronomer and mathematician Brahmagupta who lived from AD598 to 665. He decided to look at cyclic quadrilaterals – in other words a four-sided shape which has all its corners on the same circle.

Cyclic quadrilaterals can be as wonky as you like – but one cute thing about them is that the opposite angles always add up to 180°. The other cute thing is that Brahmagupta came up with this formula:

★ **Area of cyclic quadrilateral =**
$$\sqrt{(s-a)(s-b)(s-c)(s-d)}$$
where $s = \frac{1}{2}(a + b + c + d)$

Yippee! We've got another cow which means semiperimeters have come up again, this time for a four-sided shape. Of course, the circle that all the corners touch is the circumscribed circle, so here's the formula for the radius. What do you think of it?

$$\star R = \frac{1}{4} \times \sqrt{\frac{(ab + cd)(ac + bd)(ad + bc)}{(s-a)(s-b)(s-c)(s-d)}}$$

Oh dear. It's obvious what the cow thinks.

Sadly most quadrilaterals can't fit all their corners on to the same circle which makes things a bit more awkward. It was about 1,200 years after Brahmagupta produced his formula that a German mathematician called Bretschneider fitted it with an upgrade so that it could work out the area of *any* quadrilateral:

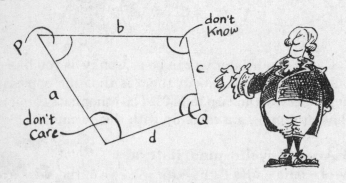

★ **Quadrilateral area =**
$$\sqrt{(s-a)(s-b)(s-c)(s-d) - abcd \times \cos^2(\tfrac{P+Q}{2})}$$

Isn't that super?

To use it you need to know all the four sides a, b, c and d, and two of the opposite angles of your quadrilateral (which are P and Q in the formula).

Just so's you know, when you get something like $abcd \times \cos^2(\tfrac{P+Q}{2})$ it's a short way to write out $abcd \times [\cos(\tfrac{P+Q}{2})]^2$. In other words you work out $\cos(\tfrac{P+Q}{2})$ and then square it before multiplying by the $abcd$ bit.

If you know the lengths of the diagonals and the angle Z between them, there is a much neater area formula:

★ **Area** $= \frac{1}{2} \times x \times y \times \sin Z$

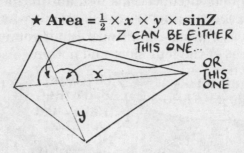

Z CAN BE EITHER THIS ONE...

OR THIS ONE

(Z can be the big angle *or* the small angle – it doesn't matter.)

Trapeziums

Trapeziums have four sides, and two of the sides are parallel. (If you're from the USA you'll call them *trapezoids*.) There is a reasonably simple formula for finding the area of a trapezium. If a and c are your parallel sides then

★ **Trapezium area** $= h\left(\dfrac{a + c}{2}\right)$

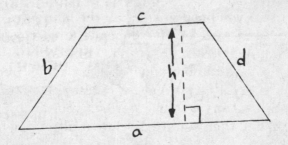

Providing you know the perpendicular height (which is the distance between your parallel lines) then it all seems quite painless enough, doesn't it? However some years ago the Murderous Maths Organization got a message asking if it was possible to work out the area of a trapezium if you just know the lengths of the four sides and nothing else.

This is a true story … well, it's *nearly* true.

We put this problem on our website and received a load of hilarious formulas which gave us the most glorious range of utterly wrong answers. However we also got two rather good formulas that we think would probably work. There was just one problem when we put them to our panel of experts…

These formulas made our heads hurt so much that it was a huge relief when we got another one from Hu Yi Jie in Singapore which we did manage to check, authorize and generally agree on:

$$\star \textbf{ Area of trapezium} = \frac{(a+c)}{4(a-c)} \times$$
$$\sqrt{(a+b-c+d)(a-b-c+d)(a+b-c-d)(-a+b+c+d)}$$

Sides a and c are parallel and a is longer than c and in case you were wondering, this is a LOT simpler than the formulas from Jenny and Carl! You can see where it comes from at *www.murderousmaths.co.uk.* and the good news is that the explanation involves a semiperimeter-escaping cow.

BIZARRE BOXES

You've already seen how complicated formulas can get when we're just dealing with flat shapes – so as you might imagine things can go very strange when we start finding formulas for lumps. However we'll just try to keep to the basics and to begin with, we'll look at Euler's classic formula which works for any lump with straight edges:

$$\star \textbf{ faces + vertices = edges + 2}$$

(A "face" is a flat side and the "vertices" are the corners.)

If you shut this book and pretend it's one solid lump you'll find it has 6 faces and 8 vertices and 12 edges, so the formula works! In fact it works for ANY lump with straight edges, no matter how complicated it looks. If you don't believe it then stick a pile of different-sized boxes together and then count up all the faces, vertices and corners *very* carefully.

Cubes and cuboids

A cube is the simplest lump because all the faces are square and the edges measure a so we get:

$\star$ **Volume of a cube = a^3**

$\star$ **Total surface area = 6a^2**

$\star$ **Total length of edges = 12a**

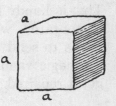

Wouldn't it be nice if all formulas were as easy as this? Sadly there aren't many cubes about these days apart from dice, but there are trillions of cuboids whose formulas aren't too tough. These are box shapes. The sides are all rectangles and the edges measure a, b and c.

★ **Volume of a cuboid**
= $a \times b \times c$

★ **Total surface area**
= $2(ab + bc + ca)$

★ **Total edges**
= $4(a + b + c)$

★ **Length of longest internal diagonal**
$x = \sqrt{a^2 + b^2 + c^2}$

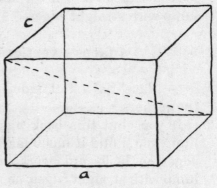

And now for three reasons why the longest internal diagonal is really useful...

1 You can work out the length of the longest stick you can pack in a box. This is handy for a conjuror who needs to send off his magic wand to get it repaired.

2 The longest internal diagonal is the diameter of the smallest sphere you can fit your box into. This is extremely useful if you urgently need to hide a box of chocolates inside a football.

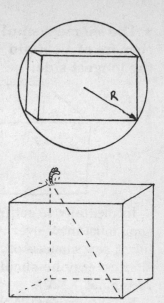

3 If you're a woodworm on one corner of a wooden block, this formula tells you how far it is to the furthest corner if you suddenly need to escape by chewing your way through the middle.

BUT WHY WOULD I NEED TO ESCAPE?

Because a woodworm-eating snail has just arrived at the corner of the block.

ARGH!

GRRR!

SLOW DEATH

As soon as the woodworm starts munching its way through, the snail decides to rush round to the far corner of the block to catch the worm when its head pops out. Of course, the question for the snail is ... what is the shortest distance it has to travel to reach the opposite corner of the block?

★ **The shortest snail trail between opposite corners of a cuboid** $= \sqrt{a^2 + (b + c)^2}$ **where a is the longest side.**

Incidentally, to get from one corner to the other, the snail must move over two of the rectangular sides. He has a few choices of which way to go, but for the shortest way he should avoid crossing the smallest rectangle!

By the way, if your block was a cube, then the longest internal diagonal works out to be $\sqrt{3} \times a$ and the shortest snail trail would be $\sqrt{5} \times a$.

Pyramids

You can start with any basic flat shape and build it up into a pyramid, and there's a very pleasing formula for the volume:

★ **Volume of pyramid** $= \frac{1}{3} \times$ **area of base** $\times$ **height**

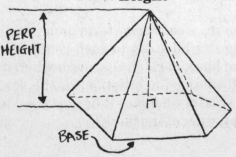

146

It doesn't matter how fancy the base of the pyramid is, so long as you know the area and the perpendicular height of the top from the base, you can get the volume.

The biggest pyramid at Giza in Egypt has a base that's 229 m square and when it was built it was 146 m high. (Since then about 10 metres got mysteriously knocked off the top.)

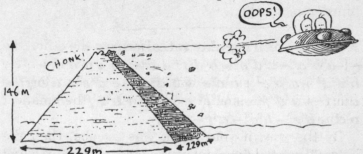

The area of the base = 229 × 229, so the volume of the pyramid used to be $\frac{1}{3}$ × 229 × 229 × 146 = 2,552,129 cubic metres.

If you don't know the perpendicular height of your pyramid then life gets a bit tough, especially if the edges are all different lengths. However if your pyramid has a triangular base then you've got a special sort of pyramid called a *tetrahedron*. It will only have six edges and each of the four faces will be a triangle.

We've already seen how Heron found a formula to get the area of a triangle just knowing the three sides without the height. This led people to wonder if you can get the area of a tetrahedron if you just know the lengths of the six edges, but not the height. WARNING! Brace yourself for this one, it's a bit scary.

147

The tetrahedron problem was solved by an early Italian Renaissance painter called Piero della Francesca. By the time he died in 1492 he had done some really nice portraits, a lot of fine religious pictures and also some *very* murderous maths...

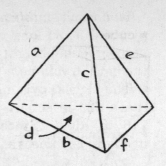

★ **Volume of irregular tetrahedron =**
$\frac{1}{12}\{-a^2b^2c^2 - a^2d^2e^2 - b^2d^2f^2 - c^2e^2\,f^2 + a^2c^2d^2 + b^2c^2d^2 + a^2b^2e^2 + b^2c^2e^2 + b^2d^2e^2 + c^2d^2e^2 + a^2b^2f^2 + a^2c^2f^2 + a^2d^2f^2 + c^2d^2f^2 + a^2e^2f^2 + b^2e^2f^2 - c^4d^2 - c^2d^4 - b^4e^2 - b^2e^4 - a^4f^2 - a^2f^4\}^{\frac{1}{2}}$

You'll see the fancy brackets { } have got a little $\frac{1}{2}$ at the end. This means that you work out everything inside the fancy brackets and then work out the square root of the LOT. Oh, and then don't forget to divide by the 12 when you've done all that.

Remember that back in Italy during the early Renaissance painters had to make their own paints. If that sounds a bit fiddly, imagine working out this formula with all those squares and then the HUGE square root bit without a calculator!

Regular solids
There are five regular solids. The edges are all the same length, and they have the same number of edges meeting at each corner. If you know which solid you've got and the side length a then you can work out their volumes and their total surface area.

solid	volume	total surface area
★ **cube**	a^3	$6a^2$

★ **tetrahedron** $\left(\dfrac{\sqrt{2}}{12}\right) \times a^3$ $\sqrt{3} \times a^2$

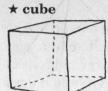

★ **icosahedron** $\left(\dfrac{5(3+\sqrt{5})}{12}\right) \times a^3$ $5 \times \sqrt{3} \times a^2$

★ **octahedron** $\left(\dfrac{\sqrt{2}}{3}\right) \times a^3$ $2 \times \sqrt{3} \times a^2$

★ **dodecahedron** $\left(\dfrac{15+7\sqrt{5}}{4}\right) \times a^3$ $3 \times \sqrt{25+10\sqrt{5}} \times a^2$

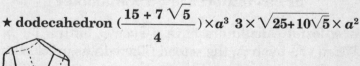

π FORMULAS

If you get ANY circle and measure the circumference then divide it by the diameter, you always get exactly the same answer which is 3·14159265358979323846264338332795 ... and it goes on for ever. As it's a bit dull writing this out, people use the strange little sign π which is called "pi".

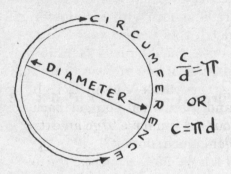

You'll see that π immediately leads to two versions of the same little formula which is one of the most important things in maths.

$$\bigstar\ \pi = \frac{\textbf{circumference}}{\textbf{diameter}}$$

or circumference = π × diameter

A lot of calculators have a special button for π. When you push it, the screen fills with as much π as will fit on so if your calculator has room for 10 digits you'll get 3·141592654. But what if you don't have a calculator with a π button? Have you got to remember 3·141592654 in your head?

The answer is NO.

How accurate do you need π to be?

If you can remember π = 3·1416 then your answers will be accurate to 99·99976%. Suppose the Earth was a perfect sphere with a diameter of 12,750 km. If you used this value of π to work out the circumference, you'd be less than 95 metres out. To give you an idea of how very accurate this is, imagine travelling the whole distance right around the equator and then when you get back to where you started you find you have to go an extra 95 metres! It doesn't seem much, does it?

π = 3·14 is 99·95% accurate and old people who don't use calculators often prefer to remember π as the fraction $\frac{22}{7}$ which is 99·96% accurate. Unless you're planning space missions, either of these will probably do you fine.

Formulas to make π

Even though there's hardly any use for lots of digits of π, hundreds of years ago people were determined to work it out as accurately as they could. Instead of measuring and dividing, they came up with the most amazing formulas in which the numbers fall into peculiar patterns. Most of these formulas go on for ever with the bits at the end getting smaller and smaller and smaller, so to make your π value more accurate, you had to stick more tiny bits on the end.

$$\frac{\pi}{2} = \frac{2}{1} \times \frac{2}{3} \times \frac{4}{3} \times \frac{4}{5} \times \frac{6}{5} \times \frac{6}{7} \times \frac{8}{7} \times \frac{8}{9} \ldots$$

John Wallis (England, 1655)

$$\frac{\pi}{6} = \frac{1}{2} + \frac{1}{2}\left(\frac{1}{3 \times 2^3}\right) + \frac{1 \times 3}{2 \times 4}\left(\frac{1}{5 \times 2^5}\right) + \frac{1 \times 3 \times 5}{2 \times 4 \times 6}\left(\frac{1}{7 \times 2^7}\right) + \ldots$$

one of Isaac Newton's (England, 1665)

$$\frac{\pi}{4} = 1 - \frac{1}{3} + \frac{1}{5} - \frac{1}{7} + \frac{1}{9} - \frac{1}{11} \ldots$$

James Gregory (Scotland, 1671)

$$\frac{\pi^2}{6} = \frac{1}{1^2} + \frac{1}{2^2} + \frac{1}{3^2} + \frac{1}{4^2} \ldots$$

just one of the many π formulas invented by Leonhard Euler from Switzerland in the eighteenth century.

So next time you prod the π button on your calculator, spare a thought for all the people who struggled through stuff like that to get the answer for you!

The bits of circles quiz and a bit of mindreading

Before we dive into all the π formulas, you have to pass a test. The distance all the way round the outside of a circle is called the circumference, but you need to know all the other names for bits of a circle. Have a look at this list and see if you can see where each bit fits on the diagrams.

a) diameter b) segment c) central angle d) sector e) arc f) chord g) centre h) radius i) tangent

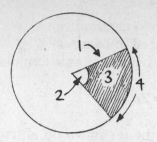 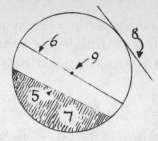

Now check your answers:

If you got all nine answers correct then give yourself a smug hug. If you only got seven answers correct then this book is going to read your mind...

RUBBISH! HOW CAN A BOOK DO THAT?

You got sector and segment the wrong way round, didn't you?

GASP!

IT'S TRUE!

Relax, we are here to help. The way to remember it is that "sector" comes from the "sentor" which is the way "centre" might have been spelt if English wasn't such a wild and crazy language.

The π formulas

Here are the letters we'll be using in the formulas:

r = radius d = diameter c = circumference

Q = central angle (measured in degrees)

Off we go then starting with a nice simple formula…

$$\star\ d = 2r$$

Ah, how lovely. Still, we better move on starting with two we know…

$$\star\ c = \pi d \text{ or } 2\pi r$$

$$\star \textbf{ Area of circle} = \pi r^2 \text{ or } \frac{\pi d^2}{4}$$

If you're a lumberjack and you don't want to be bothered with π, all you need to find out the area of a circular stump is a tape measure. You measure across the middle to get the diameter and then measure around the outside to get the circumference. Multiply them together, divide by four and you've done it.

$$\star \textbf{ The lumberjack's area of a circle} = \frac{cd}{4}$$

This last formula is handy if you've just chopped a huge tree down with a dirty great big chainsaw and you want to know the area of the exposed stump. The odd thing is that nobody has ever discovered why a lumberjack needs to know this, although several people have tried to ask.

Here are a couple more circle formulas:

★ **Length of arc =** $\dfrac{Q}{360} \times c$ **or** $\dfrac{Q}{180} \times \pi r$

★ **Length of chord** $y = 2r \times \sin\left(\dfrac{Q}{2}\right)$ **or** $2\sqrt{r^2 - h^2}$

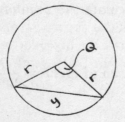 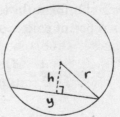

And now here comes the fun bit. We're about to do the area of a sector and the area of a segment. One is fairly easy, but the other is murderous! Which do you think will be simpler to work out? Have a guess...

The area of a sector is much easier. All we need to do is work out the area of the whole circle and then use the central angle Q to see how much of it we need. Porky Boccelli is going to let us demonstrate this by letting us cut a piece of cake for him.

Here's the formula to calculate the area on top of Porky's piece of cake:

★ **Area of sector** $= \dfrac{Q}{360} \times$ **area of circle** $= \dfrac{Q}{360} \times \pi r^2$

The area of the segment is tougher. The way the formula works it out is to calculate the area of the sector that the segment fits in, and then subtract the area of the triangle we don't need.

$$\frac{Q}{360} \times \pi r^2 \quad - \frac{1}{2}\, r^2 \sin Q$$

We've just seen the area of the sector, and if we adapt the triangle formula from page 128 you'll see the triangle area is $\frac{1}{2} r^2 \sin Q$. We end up with:

★ **Area of a segment** $= \dfrac{r^2}{2} \left(\dfrac{Q}{180}\, \pi - \sin Q \right)$

Crescents

There are two sorts of crescent shape that occur naturally, and both of them happen in the sky. The obvious one is the changing shape of the moon, and the other one is what you see when there's an eclipse. Although they are both called crescents, they are different shapes and they have VERY different area formulas. One is quite easy, but the other is ... well you'll see.

The lunar crescent

As you probably know, the moon doesn't shine on its own. We can only see it because it is lit up by the sun, and the shape of the moon we can see depends on where the sun is. The shape starts off as nothing (a new moon), then goes to the pretty crescent shape, then to a half-circle, then to the fat "gibbous" shape and finally to the complete circle shape (a full moon) before it does everything backwards until it's a new moon again. It takes about 29·5 days to go from one new moon to the next.

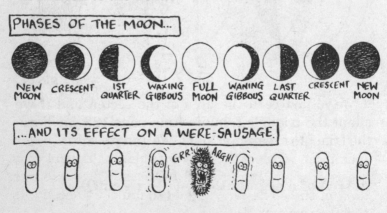

PHASES OF THE MOON...

NEW MOON · CRESCENT · 1ST QUARTER · WAXING GIBBOUS · FULL MOON · WANING GIBBOUS · LAST QUARTER · CRESCENT · NEW MOON

...AND ITS EFFECT ON A WERE-SAUSAGE.

GRR! ARGH!

The helpful thing about any moon crescent shape is that if you draw a line between the two points, it always goes through the centre of the moon's circle. (See the dotted lines in the pictures.) Now imagine another line at right angles that divides the crescent in two.

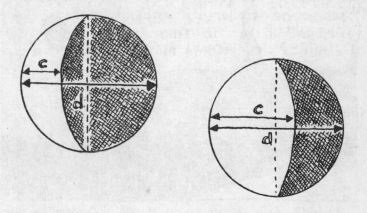

If d is the diameter of the full circle and c is the maximum width of the crescent then the area of your crescent is $\frac{c}{d} \times$ the area of the circle. Of course, the area of the circle is $\frac{\pi d^2}{4}$ so if we multiply these bits together we get:

★ The area of a lunar crescent = $\frac{1}{4}\pi cd$

That's the easy one, now get ready for trouble.

The eclipse crescent
There are two different occasions when we see eclipse crescents.

- A solar eclipse. This happens during the day when the moon passes in front of the sun. As it goes across it blocks out some of the sunlight, creating a crescent shape.
- A lunar eclipse. This happens at night when the Earth passes between the sun and the moon. At first you see a full moon, but then a black circle moves over it. This circle is the Earth's shadow.

In both cases the crescent shape is formed by one circle blocking off part of another circle. You can also make your own crescent shapes with two paper circles, one black and one white, which can be different sizes. Partially cover the white circle with the black one and you get a white crescent.

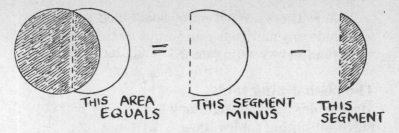

THIS AREA EQUALS   THIS SEGMENT MINUS   THIS SEGMENT

The diagram shows that we *could* work out the crescent area by working out the segment of the white circle and subtracting the segment of the black one. But the trouble is that the segment formula we saw earlier on page 157 needed an angle in the middle and here we've only got three measurements.

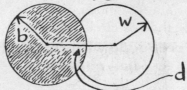

b = the radius of the black circle
w = the radius of the white circle
d = the distance between the centres of the circles.

So even though the final formula only involves subtracting one segment from the other, because we don't know any angles it's just a teeny bit more complicated...

★ **Crescent area =**

$$w^2 \left\{ \pi - \frac{2\pi \left[\cos^{-1}\left(\frac{w^2 + d^2 - b^2}{2wd} \right) \right]}{360} + \frac{\sin 2\left[\cos^{-1}\left(\frac{w^2 + d^2 - b^2}{2wd} \right) \right]}{2} \right\}$$

$$- b^2 \left\{ \frac{2\pi \left[\cos^{-1}\left(\frac{b^2 + d^2 - w^2}{2bd} \right) \right]}{360} - \frac{\sin 2\left[\cos^{-1}\left(\frac{b^2 + d^2 - w^2}{2bd} \right) \right]}{2} \right\}$$

Wahey! There are not many books that would dare to include any maths as murderous as this – so aren't you proud to be reading one?

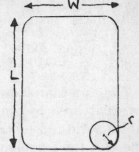

The posh dining table

Most tables are rectangular, but posh dining tables have rounded corners.

So to make your common old kitchen table posh, you just need to saw off some circular bits. If the maximum length and width of your table are l and w and the radius of the corners is r then:

★ **Area of rectangle with rounded corners =**
$$lw - r^2(4 - \pi)$$

Two formulas for the area of the white bit of a perfect fried egg

A perfect fried egg has to be perfectly circular and the yellow yolk has to be a perfect circle that's exactly in the middle. To celebrate this beautiful shape, mathematicians even gave it a special name: **annulus.**

This name applies to any big circle with a smaller circle missing out of the centre. It is also the shape of the shadow cast by a doughnut, or if you leave a very hot plate on a perfectly lovely polished wooden table top you get a misty white annulus. You also get into a LOT of trouble, so don't try it.

The area of the white bit is the same as the area of the whole big circle minus the area of the middle circle, so if the radius of the whole egg is e and the radius of the yolk is y then we get this:

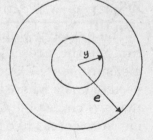

★ **The obvious area formula for the white bit of an egg:** $\pi(e^2 - y^2)$

If you see a perfect fried egg and want to work out the area of the white bit (and let's face it, who doesn't?) you need to work out where the very centre of the egg is. Then you need to take two measurements to get the radius of the yolk and then the radius of the whole egg. This is a bit like hard work so thank goodness there's an exciting formula to use instead!

The amazing thing about an annulus is that you can get the area of the white bit with just ONE measurement – and you don't need to know where the centre of the two circles is! All you do is measure across like this...

Your line should go from one edge of the egg to the other and just touch the edge of the yolk. If the length of the line is w then:

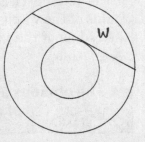

★ The exciting area formula for the white bit of an egg = $\pi(\frac{w}{2})^2$

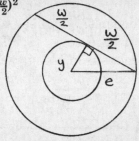

The reason for this is really lovely (if you like this sort of thing). Look at this diagram:

The line w is a tangent to the smaller circle so it meets the line y at 90°. Therefore we have a right-angled triangle. The long side measures e and the two short sides are y and half of w which is $\frac{w}{2}$. Old Pythagoras says that in a right-angled triangle the square on the hypotenuse is equal to the squares on the other two sides added together. In this case we have $e^2 = y^2 + (\frac{w}{2})^2$. If you shift this round you get $e^2 - y^2 = (\frac{w}{2})^2$.

Now if you look back to the obvious formula we have area = $\pi(e^2 - y^2)$. If we just swap the $(e^2 - y^2)$ bit for $(\frac{w}{2})^2$ we get the exciting formula.

Lumps of π

The easiest lumpy circle shape to deal with is a cylinder such as a tin can. You need to know the radius r of the base and the height h.

★ **Volume of a cylinder** = $\pi r^2 h$

If you need the surface area of a cylinder, remember there's the tube bit, and also the two ends. If you just want the area of the tube bit, you'll see that the rectangle is as long as the circumference of the base.

★ **Surface area of the tube bit of a cylinder = 2πrh**

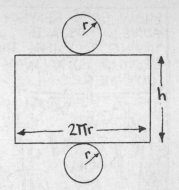

★ **Surface area of the whole cylinder including the ends = 2πr(h + r)**

People knew about these cylinder formulas thousands of years ago, but what got them stuck was the volume of a sphere. As it turns out the answer was both simple and satisfying, but it still took one of the greatest brains that ever lived to work it out. To get the full story we'll go back to Sicily in the year 212 BC.

The Romans are attacking the port of Syracuse which just happens to be the home of a 75-year-old gentleman known as Archimedes...

167

168

HE'S ONLY THE GREATEST BRAIN ON THE PLANET! HE INVENTED THE ARCHIMEDES SCREW FOR RAISING WATER, LEVERS AND PULLEYS THAT LIFT MASSIVE OBJECTS, THE SAND RECKONER, WHICH IS THE BIGGEST COMPUTING SYSTEM EVER KNOWN, GIANT CATAPULTS... IN 2.212 YEARS HE'LL EVEN GET 15 PAGES TO HIMSELF IN 'DESPERATE MEASURES' FOR INVENTING THE ARCHIMEDES PRINCIPLE!

THEY EVEN SAY HE INVENTED A RAY-GUN THAT CATCHES SUNLIGHT AND SETS FIRE TO ENEMY SHIPS!

SNIFFLE SNIFF POORP

OOPS...

TELL US, ARCHIE, OF ALL YOUR GREAT DISCOVERIES, WHICH ONE IS YOUR FAVOURITE?

IT'S...

IT'S...

URK!

DRAW DRAW

It's true. Of all his amazing discoveries, the one Archimedes was proudest of was represented by the diagram on his gravestone:

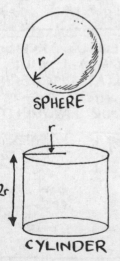

★ **The volume of a sphere = $\dfrac{4}{3}\,\pi r^3$**

What Archimedes had shown was that if you put a sphere inside the smallest cylinder that will hold it, it will take up exactly $\frac{2}{3}$ of the space. It isn't hard to see what the volume of the cylinder will be, because the height is the same as the diameter of the sphere which is $2r$. Therefore the volume of the cylinder will be $2\pi r^3$ and that makes the volume of the sphere $\frac{2}{3} \times 2\pi r^3 = \frac{4}{3}\pi r^3$.

SPHERE

CYLINDER

Here's something rather good which leads to a neat result:

★ Surface area of a sphere = $4\pi r^2$

Now for the neat bit. If you chop a sphere in half, what will the surface area be? The area of the curved bit will be half the area of the sphere so it's $\frac{1}{2} \times 4\pi r^2 = 2\pi r^2$ and the area of the flat bit will be πr^2. Therefore if you add them together you get:

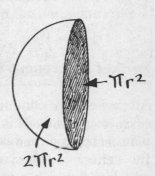

★ Surface area of a hemisphere (including the flat bit) = $3\pi r^2$

Obviously you'll want to prove this, so grab your dirty old chainsaw and chop a perfectly round orange in half and measure it. Incidentally, if you don't quite chop down the middle you'll just get the "cap" of a sphere.

Don't worry! We wouldn't leave you stranded. If you call the radius of the base of the cap x, we've got formulas for that too...

★ **Volume of the cap of a sphere** = $\frac{1}{6}\pi h(3x^2 + h^2)$
★ **Surface area of the cap of a sphere** = $2\pi rh$

Perfect ice creams, doughnuts and sausages

An ice-cream cone is a *right circular pyramid*. This means the point of the cone is directly above the centre of the circular base and like any other pyramid the volume is $\frac{1}{3} \times$ base $\times$ height.

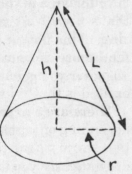

★ **Volume of a cone** = $\frac{1}{3}\pi r^2 h$

What's rather pleasing is the formula for the area of the slanting side of the cone. There are a few angles in a cone, so you might think that some miserable little SIN or TAN would be creeping in, but no! If the length of the cone from the point to the edge of the base is l then...

★ **Area of the slanting side of a cone** = πrl

Now turn your cone upside down and plonk a perfect hemispherical dollop of ice cream in it. The total volume will be...

★ **Volume of ice cream and cone** $= \frac{1}{3}\pi r^2(h + 2r)$

Now shove a flaky chocolate stick and a couple of wafers in it and then cover it in nuts and strawberry sauce. Done that? Good. Incidentally, if you still care what the formula for the volume is, you need to seek some sort of help.

Doughnuts

If you have a perfect doughnut shape, it's like a tube that's been bent round so the ends join to make a ring. This shape is called a **torus** and it gets mathematicians excited in all sorts of different ways. (Of course the main way it gets mathematicians excited is that it looks like a doughnut.)

There are two formulas for the volume of a torus, depending on what you know. We have sent Mr Reeve two warm sugar-coated doughnuts so that he can draw them and mark in what the letters r, R, a and b stand for.

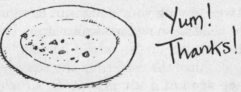

Yum!
Thanks!

We have now sent Mr Reeve two soggy pepper-coated doughnuts and let's see if we have any more luck.

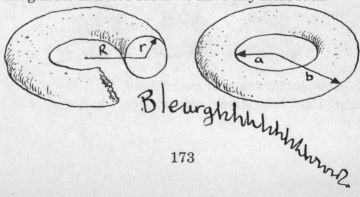

Bleurghhhhhhhhhhhhhhhh

★ **Volume of a torus** $= 2\pi^2 Rr^2$ or $\frac{\pi^2}{4}(b+a)(b-a)^2$

Wow! Did you see that? In case you missed it, we should tell you that something very rare just landed on the page. We're not talking about plain old π because that's rather common, but if you look carefully you'll see we've got the very rare lesser-spotted great crested π^2. What a treat! Truly dedicated Murderous Maths fans often spend years disguised as bushes staring down binoculars at distant sums and formulas in the hopes of spotting just one π^2, and yet you've just stumbled across two together!

If you were giving your doughnut a sugar coating, you'd also need to know the surface area. Here's what you need…

★ **Surface area of a torus** $= 4\pi^2 Rr$ or $\pi^2(b^2-a^2)$

How lucky can you get? There are *two more* π^2 formulas! Everybody remembers what they were doing when they first see a π^2 – so don't forget to tell your great-grandchildren that you were reading a Murderous Maths book and you saw four together. They'll be just sooooo jealous.

Now we'll just quietly tiptoe away and leave them in peace, we don't want to scare them away...

At last! The Tragic Tale of The Perfect Sausage
As you might recall from the start of the book, we invented the perfect sausage to make sausage calculations easier, but we had no idea that anyone would use it as an excuse to cause trouble. It all started when somebody from the Ministry of SYBNIOPB (Sticking Your Big Nose Into Other People's Business) pinched the idea from us and put it in this document:

17: a: 8f: A maximum of 29 leaves per branch (or 3 per twig).
17: b SAUSAGE: the perfect - mandatory shape of
17: b: 1: The body of the sausage should be a perfect cylinder shape
17: b: 2a: The end of the sausage should be an exact hemisphere
17: b: 2b: And the other end should also be an exact hemisphere.
17: c TOOTHPASTE: permitted flavours
17: c: 1: Cheese and onion
17: c: 2: Garlic mushroom
17: c: 3: Lard

Of course we never wanted it to be so official. All we wanted to do was present the world with these formulas:

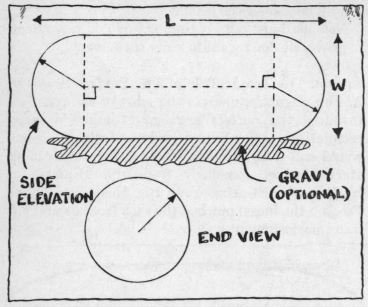

If the total sausage length = l and the width = w then:

★ **Volume of a perfect sausage** = $\dfrac{\pi w^2}{4}\left(l - \dfrac{w}{3}\right)$

★ **Area of sausage skin** = $\pi w l$

It all seemed perfectly harmless at the time, but once the official document came to the attention of the councillors in the foul city of Fastbuck, things quickly got out of control.

The Fastbuck Gazette

NEW RULES ON THE PERFECT SAUSAGE

Our beloved town council is insisting that all sausages should conform to the perfect international standards laid down by somebody that nobody's heard of with nothing better to do in an office a long, long way away. "This is important!" said the mayor. "We'll send out our inspectors immediately."

Also inside: TV guide, Celebrity Cooking tips, Hospital falls down, Sewage overflows, Crime soars, Toxic chemical leaks, Schools close, Transport chaos, Prize Crossword

To our horror, the perfect sausage had given the Fastbuck councillors a project they could really get their teeth into. They all went round checking if sausages were breaking the rules rather than worrying about more expensive problems such as collapsing hospitals and crumbling roads.

178

Of course in a tragic tale such as this, there are no winners, just losers. Everybody comes out older and perhaps a little wiser, but nobody ends up happier. And in a strange quirk of justice, the person who was most responsible for the trouble turned out to be the biggest loser of all.

The Fastbuck Gazette

SAUSAGE CRISIS OVER

At last our butcher has a new stock of sausages, so we asked if he thought the mayor was going to declare them illegal. "He hasn't complained yet," said the butcher. "In fact he was dying to help us and by the end he'd really put his heart into them."

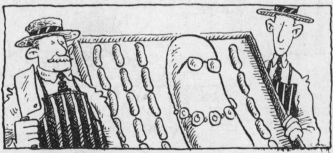

MYSTERY OF MISSING MAYOR

There's still no sign of our beloved Mayor who hasn't been seen since the new sausage rules were enforced. "He's always being invited out," said Mrs Mayor. "So maybe somebody's having him for dinner."

The ellipse mystery

An ellipse is like a squashed circle and it's rather a mysterious shape. It's easy enough to work out the area of an ellipse, you just find the smallest rectangle

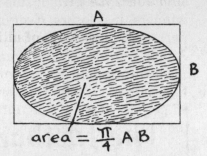

$$area = \frac{\pi}{4} AB$$

it will fit into and multiply the area by $\frac{\pi}{4}$. A is the major axis (or the width) and B is the minor axis (or the height).

★ **Area of ellipse** = $\frac{\pi}{4} AB$

However it's more common to use two measurements a and b that go from the very centre of the ellipse to the edge.

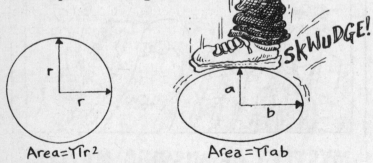

Area=πr^2 Area=πab

Suppose you start with a circle and mark in two radii at right angles. If both of them are length r then the area will be πr^2. Now when you squash the circle into an ellipse, the two radii will change length. The shortest possible radius will be a and the longest will be b. If you just swap the r^2 in the circle formula

180

for a and b you get:

★ **Area of ellipse = πab**

The mysterious bit is that nobody has yet come up with a decent formula to work out the perimeter of an ellipse! However if you're really desperate to know then here's one that's fairly close...

★ **Perimeter of an ellipse is roughly =**

$$\pi(a + b) \left(\frac{1 + \frac{3(a-b)^2}{(a+b)^2}}{[10 + \sqrt{4 - \frac{3(a-b)^2}{(a+b)^2}}]} \right)$$

Burgers and rugby balls

In the same way that an ellipse is like a squashed circle, an ellipsoid is like a squashed (or stretched) sphere. The ellipse volume formula is similar to the sphere volume formula, but the r^3 has been swapped for abc.

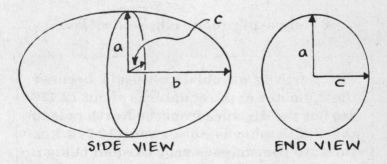

★ **Volume of ellipsoid = $\frac{4}{3}\pi abc$**

There are two special sorts of ellipsoid. If you squash a round balloon you'll get something a bit like a burger shape. From the top it looks like a circle and from the side it looks like an ellipse and this is an **oblate ellipsoid**. But if you grab your balloon at opposite sides and stretch it you'll get something more like a rugby ball. This is a **prolate ellipsoid**.

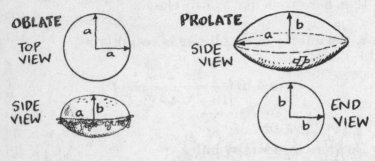

If you call the bigger measurement a and the smaller one b then...

★ **Volume of oblate ellipsoid = $\frac{4}{3}\pi a^2 b$**

★ **Volume of prolate ellipsoid = $\frac{4}{3}\pi ab^2$**

The Earth is an oblate ellipsoid because the diameter of the equator is about 12,756 km but the distance from the North pole to the South pole is only about 12,714 km. Because the shape is very close to being a sphere, it can also be called an oblate *spheroid*.

The easiest way of getting the volume of a burger or rugby ball or any other weird ellipsoid is to put it into the smallest cuboid box it will fit into. The volume of the ellipsoid is the volume of the box $\times \frac{\pi}{6}$.

One word of warning: don't get your ellipsoids muddled up.

THE CARD HOUSE AND OTHER ODD FORMULAS

The card house

It was the busiest night of the month in the Last Chance Saloon. Trail-weary cowhands leant on the bar, the variety girls were gathered around the piano, the shopkeepers and traders were clustered around the tables and the old hound dog lay in front of the fireplace – and every single one of them was holding their breath, scared to make the slightest move. Even the barman's hand had frozen in position, still holding the towel to the glass he had been wiping. Like everybody else, he was watching Riverboat Lil very cautiously arrange the very last two playing cards on the top of the card house she had been building on the green baize table.

With great delicacy she released the cards and then slowly took a step backwards.

"Ahhh!" murmured the crowd quietly.

Then the saloon door flew open, and a man in a long black coat strode in and stomped across to the bar.

"Awww!" murmured the crowd not so quietly.

"What's up?" demanded Brett Shuffler, but too late. His clumping footsteps on the old creaky floor had already shaken the table enough to bring the entire house of cards clattering down.

"Nothing's up," said Lil. "At least, it ain't now. You just knocked it all down."

Brett looked round the saloon and saw lots of disappointed people all staring at him. There was just one smile in the crowd which was on a fresh-faced young man in a slick city suit.

"I had a bet that the lady couldn't build a card house using all the cards in the place," said the stranger.

"And he was just going to pay out, too," said Lil. "But now, thanks to you, I've got to hand over fifty green ones."

Lil reached into her velvet bag and without having to look, her experienced fingers fumbled around and pulled out exactly fifty dollars which she handed to the young man.

"Well, I'll chew ma own head off!" grinned Brett reaching over to shake the young man's hand. "If you won a bet with Lil, I'm mighty pleased to meet you, stranger. The name's Shuffler, Brett Shuffler."

"Doc Watts," said the young man introducing himself. "But I got to say, it seems mighty unfair to be taking her money when it was you that brought all the cards down."

A deep murmur of agreement rumbled around the room making Brett feel embarrassed. The variety girls sniffed disapprovingly and the cowhands' eyes glared out from under the brims of their hats. He realized they all thought he should offer to pay Lil's bet, but as she'd won so much money from him in the past, he had no intention of doing so.

"So, what line of business are you in then, Doc?" asked Brett lightly, trying to change the subject.

"I'm a Doc," said the Doc, making Brett feel stupid as well as embarrassed. "I can cure anything with my Miracle Wonder Medicine."

 Everybody stretched their heads to see as the young doctor reached into his carpet bag and pulled out an armful of corked bottles.

"It comes in two types," continued the Doc. "Pink and yellow. The pink cures your insides and the yellow cures your outsides."

"What's that stuff made from?" asked Brett.

"Aha!" said the Doc. "It's a secret formula known only to me and my grandpappy. And he's dead."

"Sounds pretty dodgy to me!" guffawed Brett. He looked around the room hoping for some support. "You wouldn't catch me buying any of that formula stuff. Mind you, if you've got a secret formula that mends card houses, Lil sure could use some right now."

"I can't mend card houses," admitted the Doc, "but I got a secret formula that tells me how many cards the lady used to build it."

Brett looked down at the floor where a mass of cards from several different packs lay scattered all around.

"Impossible!" said Brett. "A secret formula can't do that."

"Hey!" said the Doc. "You callin' me a liar? I tell you ALL my formulas work. You wanna take a bet on it?"

Everybody was looking at Brett expectantly. They had all heard his dispute with the young stranger, and they wanted to see justice done.

"Go on, Brett," said Lil. "Put your money where your big mouth is. If he can tell us how many cards there are using his formula, then you apologize and you buy all his Miracle Wonder Medicines."

"Maybe he counted all the cards as you were puttin' them up," said Brett.

"Aw, stop sheepin'," said Lil. "Besides, I started building it before he even came in. All he saw was that it was thirteen layers of cards high."

"But every layer needs a different number of cards!" gasped Brett. "So that doesn't tell anybody anything."

"It's all my formula needs," said the Doc.

"Is it?" asked Brett.

"Sure is," said the Doc.

"Is it?" asked everybody.

"Sure is," said the Doc.

"Woof?" asked the old hound dog.

"Sure is," said the Doc. "So have we got a bet? I'm sayin' that my formula can work out how many cards there are before you can count them."

Brett grinned. He didn't know much about

187

formulas, but he did know that he could count mighty fast.

"You just got yourself a bet, mister!" he said.

The whole bar cheered as Brett dropped to his knees and began scooping up the cards, frantically counting them as he did so. Behind him, Doc Watts casually sat down and pulled out a small pad of paper.

"Anyone got a pencil?" he asked.

"Be my guest," smiled Lil, taking a thin eyebrow liner from her bag and passing it over.

"I'm nearly done here!" grinned Brett, reaching for the last three cards. "Two-fifty-seven, two-fifty-eight ... TWO HUNDRED AND FIFTY-NINE!"

"Nearly," said the Doc, checking his piece of paper. "The answer is two hundred and sixty."

"You sayin' I'm wrong?" said Brett. "But I counted them!"

"I'm saying you're wrong too, Brett," said Lil.

"How do you know?" they both said.

"I used exactly five packs of 52 cards," said Lil. "Makes two-sixty just like the Doc said."

"So how come I only counted two-fifty-nine?" demanded Brett, rising to his feet.

The crowd laughed and jeered. Brett looked down to see he had been kneeling on the four of hearts.

"Aw, shoot ma boot!" cursed Brett who passed over his wallet as Doc Watts happily handed over all his coloured bottles.

"Look on the bright side, Brett," laughed Lil. "With all that miracle formula, you ain't ever gonna have another sick day in your entire life!"

So what was Doc Watt's secret formula?

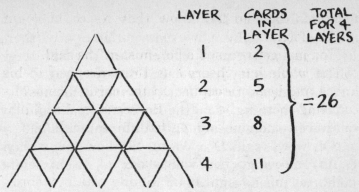

LAYER	CARDS IN LAYER	TOTAL FOR 4 LAYERS
1	2	
2	5	
3	8	= 26
4	11	

If your card house is built the usual way, then the top layer will just have 2 slanting cards. The next layer needs one flat card and four slanting cards. The third layer needs two flat cards and six slanting cards and so on.

★ **Cards required for card house =** $\dfrac{l(3l + 1)}{2}$

where l = number of layers

"Neat formula!" said a voice from the crowd. Another young man stepped forward wearing a flat hat and a kindly smile. "I'm the Reverend Joachim, and I've got my own formula about dominoes."

"Let's break out a box and see what the good man says," said Lil.

The barman passed a box of dominoes over and soon they were spread out all over the green baize table. The Reverend removed all the "doubles" and left the others all face up.

"You take any number of dominoes," said the Reverend, "and lay them in a line end to end."

"I got four dominoes," said Brett.

189

"I got five," said Lil.

"Then I can tell you how many different ways there are of laying them in a line!" said the Reverend. "Brett, you can lay yours in 384 different ways."

"384?" gasped Brett. "With just four dominoes?"

"That's nothing," said the Reverend. "Lil could lay out her five dominoes in 3,840 different ways."

"Oh wow!" said Doc Watts. "So how many ways could I arrange the whole box of twenty-eight dominoes in a straight line?"

"That could take a while to figure out," admitted the Reverend Joachim.

The Reverend's formula combines two things – the *position* of each domino and the *orientation* of each domino.

Position: when you place each domino in the line you can lay them in any order. This is the same as permutations (see page 103), so if you have 3 dominoes, you can lay them in 3! = 3 × 2 × 1 = 6 different ways.

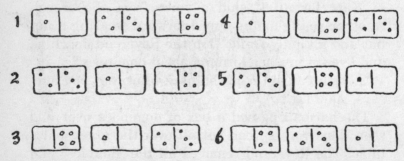

Therefore if you have *n* dominoes, the number of permutations is *n*!

Orientation: once each domino is in position, it can have two different orientations – in other words it can be placed two different ways round. If you have one domino there are $2^1 = 2$ ways it can lie. If you have two dominoes there are $2^2 = 4$ ways they can lie.

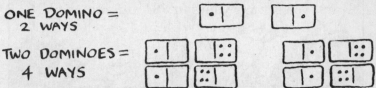

ONE DOMINO =
2 WAYS

TWO DOMINOES =
4 WAYS

The number of orientations of n dominoes is 2^n.

When you put the position and orientation together you find that the number of ways you can lie n different dominoes in a straight line is given by:

★ **The Reverend's domino formula = $2^n \times n!$**

The "doubles" cause problems because they only have one orientation.

However we can adjust the formula to allow for doubles. If you have a selection of different dominoes which includes d doubles then the number of ways of laying them in a straight line is $2^{(n-d)} \times n!$

A normal set of dominoes ranging from double blank to double six has 28 dominoes, and seven of them are doubles. Therefore using the formula, the number of different ways you can lie a normal set of dominoes in a straight line is...

$$2^{(n-d)} \times n! = 2^{(28-7)} \times 28! = 2^{21} \times 28! =$$
$$639{,}397{,}201{,}679{,}144{,}945{,}978{,}450{,}116{,}608{,}000{,}000$$

Unit fractions

In *The Mean and Vulgar Bits* it tells you that the ancient Egyptians liked working with "unit fractions" which always have a 1 on the top. Instead of saying $\frac{2}{7}$ they would say $\frac{1}{4} + \frac{1}{28}$. Sunny (our Slovenian correspondent) showed us the system she uses for converting fractions to unit fractions:

$$\star \quad \frac{a}{b} = \frac{1}{w+1} + \frac{a-r}{(w+1)b}$$

$\frac{a}{b}$ is the fraction you want to convert. To get w and r you need to divide b by a. The answer will give you a whole number (w) and a remainder (r). If you remember the "day of the week algorithm" on page 95, then $w = [\frac{b}{a}]$ and $r = (b)\text{MOD}a$.

Suppose you want to convert $\frac{3}{17}$. $a = 3$ and $b = 17$. Next you work out $b \div a$ which is $17 \div 3$ and you get 5 with a remainder of 2. Therefore $w = 5$ and $r = 2$. Now you just plonk everything into the formula to get:

$$\frac{3}{17} = \frac{1}{5+1} + \frac{3-2}{(5+1)17} = \frac{1}{6} + \frac{1}{102}$$

This formula gives you two fractions and the first one is always a unit fraction. If the second fraction is not a unit fraction then you need to use the same method on it and keep going. Don't get too carried away though or you'll find yourself working out things like this:

$$\frac{17}{19} = \frac{1}{2} + \frac{1}{3} + \frac{1}{17} + \frac{1}{388} + \frac{1}{375972}$$

The clock-face protractor
If ever you're at a monster rave party and the music system melts, you could always keep the atmosphere pumped up by demonstrating this delightful little formula:

★ The angle between the two hands of a clock = (5·5m – 30h)°

where m = minutes and h = hours. Ignore any minus signs in the answer!

So at 4:50 the angle between the hands is (5·5 × 50 – 30 × 4) = (275 – 120) = 155°.

Celsius, Fahrenheit and Kelvins

These days nearly everybody measures temperature using the Celsius or Centigrade scale (°C). However old people still use Fahrenheit (°F) so here's how to turn one into the other.

$$\bigstar \; C = (F - 32) \times \frac{5}{9} \;\text{ and }\; F = \frac{9C}{5} + 32$$

Boiling point of water: 100°C = 212°F
Freezing point of water: 0°C = 32°F
Normal blood temperature 37°C = 98·6°F
A perfectly useless fact –40 °C = –40 °F

Averting conversion confusion

Most conversion formulas just involve one little sum which is either multiplying or dividing, but people often don't know which to do. Here is one of the most basic conversion formulas which turns old-fashioned inches into centimetres:

★ **1 inch = 2·54 cm**

The number "2·54" is the conversion factor and to convert inches to centimetres you just multiply by it. If your bed is 78 inches long, then to get the length in cm you work out 2·54 × 78 = 198·12 cm.

But suppose you know you're 155 cm tall. To find your height in inches you use the conversion factor, but do you multiply or divide? The trick is to think to yourself: "Should the answer be more or less?" Inches are bigger than centimetres, so your answer should have fewer of them. Therefore your height in inches is 155 ÷ 2·54 = 61 inches. Hooray! That means you should be able to fit into your 78-inch bed and you'll have enough room to snuggle up to your geometry set. (Warning – keep the lid on. There's spiky bits inside.)

Of course if you accidentally multiplied instead of divided, then your height would work out to be 155 × 2·54 = 393·7 inches. Good night, and sleep *very* tight.

Here are a few more common conversion factors:

1 mile = 1·61 km 1 metre/second = 3·6 km/hour
= 2·24 miles/hour
1 pint = 0·568 litres 1 pound (weight) = 0·454 kg

Conversions are especially important when you're dealing with...

Foreign money

Suppose you've got £100 to take on holiday and you want to know how much foreign money you can get. What you need to know is the *exchange rate* and you use this formula:

**★ Amount of foreign currency you get =
exchange rate × your money**

Suppose the exchange rate is 2·6 Forrins to the £, then you should get 2·6 × £100 = F260. (Do bear in mind that whoever changes the money might charge you for doing it so you may get less than your F260.)

Impossible additions

Foreign money can give you a whole set of extra problems if you ever have the misfortune to go shopping at Fiendish Supplies on the Miser Isles. The only currency that the  proprietor accepts is the Fleess which only has two different coins.

This means that you can't pay exactly for anything that costs 1F, 2F, 4F, 5F, 7F, 10F or 13F. The fun bit is that you can check this with the McCullough formulas which tell you H: the highest amount you can't make from the coins and C: the total number of different amounts you can't make.

$$\star\; H = xy - x - y \text{ and } C = \frac{(H + 1)}{2}$$

where x and y are the values of your two coins.

(Note: The values of the coins must be *relatively prime*, in other words there should not be a number that will divide into both of them. If your coins are 9F and 15F this formula won't work because both values divide by 3.)

As our coins have values 3F and 8F, then we can check $H = (3 \times 8 - 3 - 8) = 13$. This means that the highest amount you can't make exactly is 13F, but you can make any other amount higher than this.

We've already seen that there are 7 amounts that you can't make exactly, and we can check this with $C = \frac{13+1}{2} = 7$.

This formula also helps if you have two values of stamps, and you need to know what other values you can make by sticking combinations of them together. If the stamps are valued at 15p and 23p, then you can work out that $H = 15 \times 23 - 15 - 23 = 307$. Therefore you can use the stamps to put the correct value on anything that costs £3.07 or more to post.

Lightning distance

When you see a lightning flash there is usually a short delay before the sound of the thunder reaches you. You can tell how far away the lightning is by counting the seconds (s) between the flash and the bang. You also need to have a rough idea how warm it is because that affects the speed of sound. Here are two approximate results:

★ **Distance to lightning in metres = s × 332 (cold day 0°C)**

★ **Distance to lightning in metres = s × 344 (warmer day 20°C)**

So roughly speaking, if the delay is 3 seconds then the lightning is about 1 km away. If the delay is 5 seconds it's about 1 mile away.

And if there's no delay at all then...

Noughts and crosses

Although the old game is usually played on a 3 × 3 grid, you can play it on a grid of any size! So if you're playing on a grid that measures $g \times g$, thank goodness for the formula that tells you...

★ **Number of possible winning lines = 2(g + 1)**

How many people hear bad jokes?

Sometimes you get a joke that is so funny that everybody who hears it tells it to everybody they know, and soon everybody on the planet knows it and keeps repeating it to everybody else. This is very dangerous because eventually every single person in the whole world is either trying to tell the joke, or looking very fed up and saying, "I've already heard it". This means that no one has time to do anything else and it leaves the planet wide open to an alien invasion.

It's because good jokes are so dangerous that the Murderous Maths Organization takes great care to ensure that none of the jokes in these books are at all funny.

Luckily bad jokes are much safer. Suppose you have a joke that is so poor that even if 100 people hear it to start with, between them they only tell 70 other people. In this case the number of people told is 0·7 × the number of people who first heard it.

As 0·7 of the people that heard the joke passed it on, this is called the **spread factor** of the joke. (So long as the spread factor is lower than 1, then the joke eventually dies out. The poorest jokes have the lowest spread factors.) Of the 70 new people to hear the joke, they will pass it on to 0·7 × 70 = 49 new people, and then they will pass it on to 0·7 × 49 new people … etc. until the joke dies out.

If s is the spread factor of the joke and the number of people who first heard it is p then:

★ The total number of people that will ever hear the joke = $\frac{p}{1-s}$

If 100 people hear a joke of spread factor 0·7, then the total number of people to suffer before the joke dies away will be $\frac{100}{1-0\cdot7} = 333$.

Density (and will things float?)

Density is how heavy stuff is, for instance solid iron is denser than polystyrene. It can be measured in kg per cubic metre written as kgm^{-3}.

$$\star \text{ Density} = \frac{\text{mass}}{\text{volume}}$$

If you have a cube of strange purple plastic that weighs 30 kg and measures 0·25 m along each side, the density = $\frac{30}{0·25^3}$ = 1,920 kgm^{-3}. We can use this to see if the cube will float on water. The density of water = 1000 kgm^{-3} and if something is less dense than this then it will float. However our plastic cube has a bigger density than water so it will sink.

Range

Back on page 59 we left Urgum the Axeman wondering how to fire his cannon without the ball landing on his foot, and at last he has realized that he needs to tilt the barrel over a bit. As he's on a flat piece of ground, there is a formula to work out the range r – in other words how far away the ball will land. You need to know the muzzle velocity v of your cannon and the angle E of elevation between the barrel and the ground.

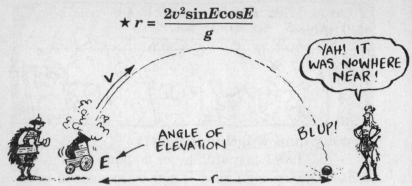

$$\star \, r = \frac{2v^2 \sin E \cos E}{g}$$

If Urgum knew about SIN and COS then he could work out the range for any angle, but as Urgum is just interested in the maximum possible range, he really ought to check the instructions.

For maximum range, set ye barrel to 45°

If there's no wind then 45° always gives the maximum range for cannons. The good bit is that SIN45° and COS45° are both equal to $\frac{1}{\sqrt{2}}$ and this gives a lovely simple formula for the maximum range of cannons:

$\star$ **maximum range of a cannon at 45°** $= \frac{v^2}{g}$

So if the Bombastic Decimator's muzzle velocity is

70 mps, then the maximum range will be $\frac{70^2}{10}$ = 490 metres.

Fibonacci numbers

The Fibonacci series starts 1, 1, 2, 3, 5, 8, 13 ... and each number is the previous two numbers added together. But what do you do if you want the 53rd number in the series? Have you got to work out all the numbers that come in front of it? No, because there's a special formula to work out any number in the series:

★ **The nth term of the Fibonacci series =**

$$\frac{1}{\sqrt{5}} \left[\left(\frac{1 + \sqrt{5}}{2} \right)^n - \left(\frac{1 - \sqrt{5}}{2} \right)^n \right]$$

The weird thing about this formula is that even though it is stuffed with $\sqrt{5}$s, somehow it always gives you an exact whole number for the answer! However you can get the answer much faster by just working out:

★ **The FAST Fibonacci n^{th} term formula =**
$(1{\cdot}618)^n \div \sqrt{5}$

... and then you round off to the nearest whole number.

And FINALLY – the Quadratic Formula

Even if this book was the size of a washing machine, there wouldn't be enough space to squeeze every possible formula into it, so we had to decide which one to finish with. We've chosen one of the greatest bits of maths of all time because it can solve ugly things called quadratic equations:

$$\star\ x = \frac{-b \pm \sqrt{b^2 - 4ac}}{2a}$$

where $ax^2 + bx + c = 0$

As you might imagine, it's rather specialized and if you're interested you can find out all about it in *The Phantom X*. The odd thing is that all sorts of old people have a strange affection for it because they remember it from school and can still recite it.

A - ONE - TWO - THREE - FOUR...

"*x* equals minus *b* plus or minus the square root of *b* squared minus four *ac* all over two *a*."

Touching, isn't it? Especially when you realize that most of them never understood what it was about in the first place. Sadly we haven't got any room left to explain it here because the last few pages of the book are reserved for an important end bit.

Ready? Then here it comes…

THE IMPORTANT END BIT

INDEX

Most of the features in this book are dealt with in more detail in the other Murderous Maths books or at *www.murderousmaths.co.uk*